FREE TRADE AND THE ENVIRONMENT

FREE TRADE

AND THE ENVIRONMENT

Mexico, NAFTA, and Beyond

Kevin P. Gallagher

STANFORD LAW AND POLITICS
An Imprint of Stanford University Press
Stanford, California 2004

Stanford University Press
Stanford, California
© 2004 by the Board of Trustees
of the Leland Stanford Junior University. All rights reserved.

Printed in the United States of America on acid-free, archival-quality paper.

Library of Congress Cataloging-in-Publication Data

Gallagher, Kevin, 1968-
  Free trade and the environment : Mexico, NAFTA, and beyond / Kevin P. Gallagher.
     p. cm.
  Includes bibliographical references and index.
  ISBN 0-8047-5065-3 (cloth : alk. paper) — ISBN 0-8047-5125-0 (pbk. : alk. paper)
  1. Free trade—Environmental aspects—Mexico. 2. Air—Pollution—Mexico. 3. Mexico—Environmental conditions. 4. Environmental policy—Mexico.   I. Title.
  HF1776.G28 2004
  363.73'0972—dc22
                                                                2004009253

Typeset by Interactive Composition Corporation in 10/13.5 Sabon
Original Printing [2004]

Last figure below indicates year of this printing:
13   12   11   10   09   08   07   06   05   04

Contents

Tables

Figures

Acknowledgments

Although this study was conducted entirely by me, I have benefited from the help of a number of individuals and institutions.

First and foremost, I am indebted to Frank Ackerman, Director of the Research and Policy Program at the Global Development and Environment Institute (GDAE) of Tufts University. Frank read and commented on numerous drafts of this book. John Kenneth Galbraith has said that he continues to hear Henry Luce make recommendations over his shoulder, even though he worked with Luce over sixty years ago. For the rest of my life, Frank will be my Henry Luce.

A special thanks goes to Daniel Esty, Yale School of Forestry, who also commented on the full manuscript. Before going to Yale, Dan was closely involved in the NAFTA negotiations as a senior member of the United States Environmental Protection Agency (EPA). Since that time, he has gone on to become one of the most well-known and highly regarded academics in the burgeoning field of trade and environment. His practical experience and scholarly expertise have proved to be of enormous help throughout this study.

Thanks also goes to William Moomaw, co-director of GDAE, and Peter Winn, also at Tufts. William and Peter read the manuscript in its entirety and provided valuable insights.

The advice and support of the Program for Science, Technology and Development (PROCIENTEC) at El Colegio de Mexico was key to the successful completion of this study and book. Alejandro Nadal and Francisco Aquayo in particular were of immense help. PROCIENTEC took me in as a visitor at their institute numerous times between 1999 and 2002. With their guidance, I obtained much of the data to perform this analysis. During this process, I not only gained colleagues, but friends.

I would also like to thank other colleagues here at GDAE. Regina Flores, Eliza Waters and Jordana Fish of GDAE played strong roles as research assistants. Tim Wise has followed this study from its inception and has offered invaluable advice, encouragement, constructive criticism, and comic relief throughout.

Other people, in no particular order, that commented on earlier draft chapters or presentations of preliminary findings are Jonathan Fox, Chantal Line Carpentier, Claudia Schatan, Alice Amsden, Mario and Luisa Molina, Samudra Vijay, Neva Goodwin, Scott Vaughan, Konrad Von Moltke, Jonathan Harris, Ann Helwege, and David Barkin. Thank you.

No part of this study and the resulting book could have been done without funding. I sincerely thank the following foundations and institutions for supporting this research: the Rockefeller Brothers Fund, the C. S. Mott Foundation, the William and Flora Hewlett Foundation, and the North American Commission for Environmental Cooperation.

I also thank Kate Wahl and others at Stanford University Press for their help and commitment.

In many ways, what led me to pursue this kind of research was the early tutelage of the late biologist Francis Crisley. Early in my career, Dr. Crisley showed me the importance of examining the interactions between the economic and ecological realms of planet earth.

To me, love and family are the core inspiration for life's work. I thank my parents, Robert and Norma Gallagher, for the upbringing and education that they gave and continue to give me. Without them none of this would be possible.

This book is dedicated to my wife, Kelly Sims Gallagher. Kelly's love—and my love for her—gives me the courage and vision to pursue this life.

1 Mexico and the Trade and Environment Debates

By autumn 1993, the U.S. government was steeped in heated negotiations over the establishment of the World Trade Organization (WTO), and in supplemental environmental accords to the North American Free Trade Agreement (NAFTA). The potential negative effect of new trade agreements on the environment was among the most contentious issues of these debates. Many environmentalists pointed to the Mexico-U.S. border (a heavily polluted area where U.S. firms have been allowed duty free imports for decades) as an example of what would happen to the rest of Mexico and other developing countries if the WTO and NAFTA came into effect.

As discussion became increasingly polarized, *Scientific American* asked two leading economists to set the record straight. The November 1993 issue of *Scientific American* became an instant classic that is now required reading in many college classrooms. The two experts were Jagdish Bhagwati (a prominent trade economist from Columbia University) and Herman Daly (a well-known environmental economist then working at the World Bank). The two authors were not in agreement. Bhagwati argued that agreements such as NAFTA would raise incomes in developing countries to a point where governments would begin to protect the environment. Daly argued that free trade would provide an incentive for heavily polluting industries in developed countries such as the United States to move their operations to developing countries where pollution control was more inexpensive and lax. Today, more than 10 years later, the trade and environment debates remain contentiously divided along the lines outlined by these two economists.

The economic transformation of Mexico, from a relatively closed, import-substituting economy before 1985, to a major trading nation today, offers the opportunity to empirically examine the extent to which authors Bhagwati and Daly were correct. Hence, the central research question for this book is: To what extent has economic integration affected levels of environmental degradation in Mexico? The time period under consideration for this analysis is 1985 to 1999. Mexico began integrating itself with the world economy in 1985, and, by 1999, it had become one of the more open economies in the world (1999 was also the most recent year of consistently available data).

Specifically, the analyses presented in this book test the Environmental Kuznets Curve hypothesis and the pollution haven hypothesis. Bhagwati argued the Kuznets curve logic, and Daly argued the pollution haven logic. A case study of criteria air pollutants in Mexican manufacturing examines what are called the scale, composition, and technique effects of economic integration. Manufacturing is examined for two reasons. First, although manufacturing emissions in Mexico form a significant share of total emissions, vehicular emissions have received the most attention. Second, newly available data on criteria air pollution in Mexican manufacturing is used throughout this study. Many studies of Mexico's environment examine either Mexico City or the U.S.-Mexico border region. This study represents the first comprehensive work to examine the Mexican economy as a whole.

To date, the data does not confirm either Bhagwati or Daly's predictions. Despite modestly rising incomes, many environmental problems worsened significantly when Mexico integrated with the world economy. The environment, however, has not worsened due to a mass migration of heavily polluting firms from the United States to Mexico. The percentage of dirty industry in the Mexican economy actually declined. What caused increased levels of environmental degradation was the lack of adequate attention by the government of Mexico, and to a certain extent the United States, to correct the market failures related to environment that arose as a result of the integration process. Such degradation has come at great cost for Mexico. According to the Mexican government, the economic costs of environmental degradation during this period averaged 10 percent of gross domestic product (GDP) per annum. That figure stands in stark contrast to the annual rise in economic growth, which was only 2.6 percent.

This study underscores the importance of making environmental protection part and parcel of the economic integration process. Developing country governments need not fear that linking environmental protection to trade liberalization will hurt their prospects for economic growth. The fact that Mexico did not serve as a depository for heavily polluting firms from the United States suggests that the costs of compliance with environmental protection are not large enough to affect plant location decisions for the majority of firms. It appears that, if developing countries erect the appropriate environmental standards, they will not scare away foreign investment during the process. Moreover, this study suggests that when firms in developed countries argue that a new or existing environmental regulations may cause them to move overseas they may be bluffing. Thus, there is no reason why environmental standards can't improve in developed countries as well.

This chapter introduces the trade and environment debate and the theoretical lenses through which economists and other analysts have begun to examine it. It also provides an outline of the argument that will be advanced later in the book, as well as a summary of the rest of the book and its findings.

Theoretical Approaches to Trade and Environment

In recent decades, the world economy has undergone an unprecedented level of integration. Since the mid-1980s, the value of world trade has more than quadrupled and the value of foreign investment has increased by a factor of 15 (UNCTAD 2002). These flows have been facilitated by a proliferation of global, regional, and bilateral trade and investment agreements. The 1990s alone ushered a new round of global trade negotiations under the General Agreement on Tariffs and Trade (GATT) that resulted in the creation of the World Trade Organization (WTO), the solidification of common markets in Europe and South America, and the NAFTA. This trend has not stopped. A new round of WTO negotiations has been launched (the Doha round), as well as a proposed Free Trade Area of the Americas (FTAA) that would integrate the economies of the Western Hemisphere. Although many analysts doubt that it is politically possible, both of these negotiations are scheduled for completion in 2005.

Alongside these trends, the environmental ramifications of trade and investment liberalization have become an area of great concern (Esty 1994). Every official meeting on the world economy has been paralleled by large-scale protests where environmental issues loom large in the opposition. Also around these meetings (or at least in reaction to or in preparation for them) is a growing but disparate set of scholars who are trying to address these issues through a more rigorous theoretical and empirical lens. This study uses a number of current theoretical perspectives in order to develop an empirically-based understanding of what has happened in Mexico. The results are sure to have implications for theory, and for future negotiations of economic integration.

Although these discussions are commonly referred to as the trade and environment debates, trade has become a catch-all term that refers to a whole package of policies. This package includes: the liberalization of both trade and investment, the increase in structural adjustment programs for the least developed countries, and the decreasing role of government in developed and developing countries alike. In much of Latin America, such a package is commonly referred to as *neoliberalismo* (neoliberalism). In the United States, this phenomenon is more often called economic integration. Still others lump all these trends together as globalization. Economic integration is the preferred term for this book, but the others may creep in to avoid being redundant. Economic integration fits best because Mexico liberalized trade and investment, privatized state-owned industries, underwent structural adjustment programs, and decreased the role of the government in a series of measures dating back to 1985.

In order to develop an understanding of economic integration's effect on the environment that is both theoretically and empirically based, this study draws on two lines of analysis: first is a body of work on what has come to be called the Environmental Kuznets Curve (EKC), and second is the literature on the pollution haven hypothesis.

The EKC is commonly evoked by free trade proponents. Indeed, it was the EKC that Bhagwati referred to when he argued that trade-led economic growth would improve environmental quality in developing nations that liberalized their trade regimes. In 1955, Simon Kuznets found an inverted U-shaped curve relationship between income inequality and levels of income. In a landmark article conducted as an attempt to predict the environmental effects of NAFTA, Grossman and Krueger (1993) found a similar relationship between environmental degradation and levels of income. The large body of work that emerged after their article has become known as the EKC literature. According to the EKC, environmental degradation may sharply increase in the early stages of economic development, but a rise in per capita income past a certain turning point, initially thought to fall between $3,000 and $5,000 in 1985 purchasing power parity (PPP) terms, would gradually reduce environmental damage.

The factors that lead to environmental improvements after the turning point is reached fall into three categories: the scale, composition, and technique effects of trade-led economic growth. Scale effects occur when economic integration causes an expansion of economic activity (output). If the amount of pollution per unit of output in the economy as a whole remains unchanged during the period of economic integration and growth, but the scale of output is growing, then pollution and resource depletion will increase as well.

Composition effects occur when changes in trade policy lead nations to specialize in particular sectors, most often those where they enjoy a comparative advantage. If the amount of pollution per unit of output remains unchanged in each industry, and the integration process causes nations to specialize in less pollution-intensive economic activity, shifting away from capital to labor intensive activity for instance, then the composition of that economy will become less pollution-intensive.

If pollution per unit of output in an industry changes during the period of integration and growth such changes are referred to as technique effects. Reductions in pollution per unit of output may occur for a number of reasons. Economic growth may trigger new investment that may bring newer, cleaner technologies. It could also raise incomes to a point where governments would establish stronger environmental problems.

For these reasons, the EKC is often evoked in political negotiations. Indeed, many free trade proponents cited the work of Grossman and Krueger to argue that NAFTA would accelerate Mexico to the turning point, and that the environmental concerns of many of NAFTA's opponents would soon be alleviated. It was argued that free trade in and of itself would eventually clean the environment. Although EKC is plausible in theory, Chapter 3 shows that there is only limited empirical support for the EKC in the academic literature (Stern 1998).

Many free trade opponents evoke the pollution-haven hypothesis. The pollution haven hypothesis blends traditional trade theory with the theory of environmental externalities. The economist David Ricardo (1817) showed that, because countries face different costs to produce the same product, if each country produces (and then exports) the goods for which it has comparatively lower costs, then all parties benefit. The effects of comparative advantage (as Ricardo's notion became called) on factors of production were developed in the Heckscher-Ohlin model. This model assumes that in all countries there is perfect competition, there is the same mix of goods and services, and that factors of production (such as capital and labor) can freely move between industries. Within this rubric, the Stolper-Samuelson theorem adds that international trade can increase the price of products in which a country has a comparative advantage.

According to these trade theories, trade liberalization between two nations could lead to an increased specialization in pollution-intensive economic activity in the country with weaker environmental policies. An efficient (or optimal) environmental policy is one where the marginal social benefits of pollution are equal to the marginal cost of that increase (Baumol and Oates 1998). If a country sets its environmental policies below the efficient level (if it fails to internalize environmental externalities and thus allows market failures), the costs of producing pollution-intensive goods will be lower relative to those of a trading partner who has set optimal environmental policy. This increased ability to specialize in pollution-intensive (or natural resource intensive) industry may provide an economic incentive for pollution intensive firms to relocate to developing countries based on lower comparative costs (Anderson 1992). This phenomena is what Daly evoked in the pages of *Scientific American*, and is commonly referred to as the pollution haven hypothesis. Like the empirical work on the EKC, Chapter 3 shows that there is limited empirical support for the pollution haven hypothesis in the peer-reviewed literature (Neumayer 2001).

This logic has been extended into the regulatory realm. It has been argued that the fear of losing comparative advantage because of increasing marginal pollution costs would cause a race to the bottom in environmental regulation. Not only would firms flock to areas where pollution control costs are relatively less costly, firms would also exert downward pressure on environmental standards in nations with more optimal environmental policies, all in the name of competition (Esty 1999; Neumayer 2001). From the perspective of the country that lacks optimal environmental policies, there are concerns that such countries could be stuck at the bottom. This result could occur because nations might fear that increasing levels of environmental protections (and therefore costs) would scare away foreign investment. Nations with differing levels of environmental policy face a classic prisoner's dilemma: competitive pressures give individual countries the incentive to pursue lower environmental policy than if they worked collectively, although cooperation between the countries would result in greater welfare for all countries (Zarsky 1997; Porter 1999).

Overview: Environmental Conditions and Economic Integration in Mexico

This book empirically examines each of these theories (the EKC, the pollution haven hypothesis, and the scale, composition, and technique effects) in order to examine the extent to which economic integration has affected levels of criteria air pollution and other environmental conditions in Mexico. Contrary to both EKC and pollution haven predictions, the main empirical results are that, on a national level, a number of environmental conditions worsened in Mexico despite rising incomes, but not because dirty industry in the United States flocked there. Rather, environmental degradation worsened because the Mexican and U.S. governments did not instate effective environmental policies that would have brought the desired benefits from economic integration.

Between 1985 to 1999, Mexico installed a sweeping array of policies in order to integrate itself with the world economy. During this short period, Mexico joined the GATT, NAFTA, the Organization for Economic Cooperation and Development (OECD), and signed well over 20 bilateral and regional economic integration agreements with other nations around the world. These policies led to an about face in Mexico's trade patterns. Oil exports amounted to 80 percent of total exports in 1985, but dropped to just 10 percent by 2000. During the same period of rapid increases in trade and investment, inflation has also become tamed. However, other results have been less remarkable. For instance, on a per capita basis real gross domestic product (GDP) has grown at a rate of less than one percent annually, and inequality and poverty have worsened considerably (for a good overview of Mexico's profound transformation and its economic effects see (Middlebrook 2003).

Over this period, Chapter 2 examines the EKC hypothesis for Mexico. Mexico reached $5,000 GDP per capita in 1985, the high end of the level of income predicted by early EKC studies to trigger decreases in environmental degradation. Ironically, 1985 is precisely the year Mexico began to integrate itself with the world economy. Since 1985, Mexico has achieved modest growth. Despite this growth, chapter two shows that Mexico is yet to reach an EKC turning point for a number of pollutants, and may not for decades to come. Chapter 2 also estimates that it would take decades of the kind of growth thus far experienced before a number of key pollutants Mexico's environment begin to decrease, if they do at all.

Mexico's environment did not primarily worsen because Mexico became a pollution haven for U.S. companies. Although the share of dirty industries in the United States (as measured by marginal pollution abatements costs) did decrease between 1988 and 1998, the share of dirty industries in Mexico also declined, and more so than in the United States.

The statistical analysis performed in Chapter 3 examines the pollution haven hypothesis from a variety of perspectives. The results of this chapter suggest that the marginal costs of pollution abatement in the United States are such a relatively small expense that they are not major factors when the majority of firms are making decisions regarding their location.

Chapters 4 and 5 comprise a case study of industrial air pollution in Mexico. In these chapters the scale, composition, and technique effects of economic integration on industrial criteria air pollution are examined. Chapter 4 looks at the scale and composition effects. I find that the composition of industry became less pollution-intensive. Such declines were outstripped by the scale effect. Although the share of pollution intensive industry in the Mexican economy declined over this period, the pace of economic growth in manufacturing (which was over 4 percent per annum) was such that total criteria air pollution in manufacturing still almost doubled.

To estimate the technique effect, Chapter 5 creates a Harmonization Index that compares the criteria air pollution intensity of Mexican and U.S. manufacturing. The chapter also performs a number of simple econometric exercises that examine the extent to which energy technology and fuel use explain the relative levels of criteria air pollution intensity in the two countries. There are a handful of industries in Mexico that are cleaner than their U.S. counterparts: notably, steel and cement. Chapter 5 shows that those industries that are cleaner in Mexico than the United States tend to be those where pollution is a function of plant vintage and fuel use. Those industries that are dirtier in Mexico use more polluting fuels, and pollution is more a function of end-of-pipe technologies. While the steel and cement stories are clear successes, the share of those industries in Mexico that are cleaner than their U.S. counterparts has been shrinking by every measure.

Chapter 6 describes how Mexico has fallen short of installing effective environmental policies to address the market failures in its changing economy. Over the past 20 years, Mexico has developed a fairly elaborate set of environmental laws, institutions, and human resources. As the World Bank and others have pointed out, Mexico has not equipped its environmental regime with adequate resources to create optimal environmental policies. Since 1993, the year after NAFTA was signed, real spending and plant-level environmental inspections have both fallen by 45 percent. On an international level, the environmental side accords of NAFTA, with some exceptions, have done little to fill this gap.

Chapter 7 summarizes the key findings of this research and answers the research questions posed in this chapter. Chapter 7 also outlines the theoretical implications of the study, in addition to a number of policy parameters for Mexico and future negotiations on economic integration.

Implications for Theory and Policy

The empirical findings in this volume have profound implications for both theory and policy. The fact that this study is consistent with the peer-reviewed literature that finds limited evidence for an EKC or pollution havens reiterates the need to address environmental externalities in an optimal manner. From both theoretical and policy perspectives, Chapter 7 outlines three main lessons that can be drawn from this study:

1. **Without the proper environmental policies in place, economic integration can exacerbate environmental problems.** This book underscores the need to couple economic integration with necessary environmental policy. Developing nations fall short of establishing social and environmental policies in the face of economic integration for two reasons: because they are often in economic (and thus fiscal) crises that make few funds for social policy available; and that developing nations fear new social policies (especially environmental ones) may scare away foreign investment and domestic industry. Kym Anderson (1992) has shown that if environmental externalities are optimally internalized developing nations need not grow at the expense of the environment.

2. **Enacting environmental policies will not scare away investment.** The fact that this study, like so many others, finds no support for the pollution-haven hypothesis is good news for developed and developing countries alike. The marginal costs of pollution abatement are not significant enough to trigger firms to re-locate (or change expansion plans) from one geographical region to another. Developed and developing countries are free to pursue environmental policies of the magnitude now in effect in developed countries without putting up barriers to economic growth. Given that environmental regulations in the U.S. don't encourage dirty firms to move to Mexico, there is room for improving environmental in this country as well.

3. **There is a clear role for industrialized nations to assist less-developing countries in meeting their environmental goals.** Dani Rodrik (2001) has shown how social policy can be crowded out by integration policy in developing countries with limited fiscal capacities. This study implies that such was the case in Mexico. Although the economy and public expenditures grew, spending on the environment plummeted and the international institutions created to help Mexico meet its environmental goals was not sufficient to come to the rescue. Chapter 7 ends by making the case that developed country trading partners should make technical and financial commitments to help developing countries meet their environmental goals.

2   Environmental Kuznets Curve for Mexico?

Chapter 1 introduced the Environmental Kuznets Curve (EKC). The EKC predicts that environmental degradation can sharply increase in the early stages of economic development, but the rise in per capita income past a certain turning point may gradually reduce environmental damage in developing countries. This chapter examines the EKC hypothesis for Mexico between 1985 and 1999.

Despite per capita incomes beyond the EKC turning point range identified in early studies, this chapter shows that a number (but not all) of the important environmental conditions have significantly worsened in Mexico during this period. The chapter also shows that such damage has proven costly for Mexico, and may be jeopardizing the very goals of Mexico's economic policies. Such findings do not necessarily prove the EKC wrong. It may just be that the turning point for Mexico will come in the future. This chapter concludes by showing that at current growth rates, decades of costly environmental degradation could occur before Mexico reaches a turning point where environmental degradation will begin to decline. This chapter is divided into five parts: 1) an assessment of the EKC literature, 2) an analysis of the EKC for Mexico using data from National Institute for Statistics, Geography and Informatics (INEGI), 3) a discussion of the economic costs of environmental degradation in Mexico, 4) a projection of the timing and economic costs of future environmental damage in Mexico, and 5) a summary of the key results, as well as questions that will be addressed throughout the rest of this book.

Environmental Kuznets Curve: Empirical Evidence

The Kuznets curve gets its name from a landmark article by Simon Kuznets (1955). Kuznets hypothesized that growth in per capita income over time first increases inequality, then later decreases. Development policy-makers evoked this theory for decades to argue that inequality could be ignored in the short term. At this writing, empirical evidence for the Kuznets curve has faded, leading economists to conclude that "there is no empirical tendency whatsoever in the inequality-development relationship" (Esty 1994; Fields 1995).

In a landmark study that attempts to estimate the environmental impact of the North Atlantic Free Trade Agreement (NAFTA) in Mexico, Grossman and Krueger (1993) reported a similar relationship between environmental degradation and levels of income: the Environmental Kuznets Curve. EKC theory states that, as countries begin to raise incomes, rates of natural resource depletion and environmental pollution will proceed rapidly. At higher levels of income, the scale, composition, and technique effects can combine to trigger a decline in environmental degradation. New forms of cleaner technology, compositional shifts toward less destructive economic activity, and pressure from newly concerned citizens can lead to improved environmental conditions. This chapter is a test of hypothesis set forth in Grossman and Krueger's initial study.

The EKC has developed into a wide literature that is not well understood in policy circles. It has now become common for policy-makers to evoke the EKC while arguing that nations should integrate their economies now and worry about the environment later. Such claims are at odds with the peer-reviewed literature on the EKC. As with the original Kuznets curve, a growing number of economists are finding an ambiguous relationship between economic growth and the environment.

The basic EKC relationship, often referred to as an inverted-U, is illustrated in Figure 2.1. The turning point where early EKC studies predicted that environmental degradation may begin to decline was found to fall between $3,000 to $5,000 Gross Domestic Product (GDP) per capita

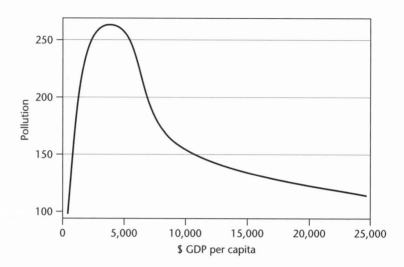

FIGURE **2.1**   The Environmental Kuznets Curve

in 1985 Purchasing Power Parity (PPP) terms. The first EKC study, by Grossman and Krueger (1993), examined ambient concentrations of sulfur, smoke, and particulate matter. They found turning points between $4,000 and $5,000 for sulfur and smoke, and an even lower turning point for particulates. Early EKC analyses were also published as part of the World Bank's *World Development Report* (1992). In that report, the turning points for ambient concentrations of sulfur and particulate matter ranged from $3,000 to $4,000 GDP per capita[1]. Such an income level is quite close to mean global income. Many free trade proponents have generalized from the EKC to argue that the environment can wait, because economic growth will eventually (and naturally) result in environmental improvements. According to the academic literature, such claims are often misconstrued. Five qualifications characterize the empirical evidence on the EKC (for comprehensive reviews see (Stern 1998):

- **Evidence for an EKC is limited to a small number of pollutants.** Thus far, evidence for an EKC relationship has been consistently found for ambient concentrations of localized air pollutants in Organization for Economic Cooperation and

1. The majority of studies are carried out using 1985 (PPP) dollars for comparative purposes.

Development (OECD) countries. EKCs have been identified for pollutants such as sulfur and particulate matter. It is thought that the EKC relationship may exist for such (criteria) pollutants because their effects are more localized and subject to regulation (Grossman and Krueger 1993; Seldon 1994; Panayotou 1997). A number of studies, however, have shown that, while ambient concentrations may decline with income, emissions increase along with income (Stern 2001). In addition to emissions, for many other environmental problems such as water pollution, municipal waste, carbon dioxide, and energy use, evidence of an EKC relationship is questionable (Bank 1992; World Bank 1992; Shafik 1994; Dua 1997; Horvatth 1997; Hettige 2000; Seldon 1994; Kaufmann 1998; List and Gallet 1999).

– **Evidence for the EKC is limited to the experience of developed nations.** Most of the studies that have found an inverted-U relationship have datasets that are dominated by or rely solely on OECD countries. In the smaller number of studies that are representative of the developing nations, evidence for an inverted-U relationship has been ambiguous (Stern, 1998; Stern and Common, 2001).

– **The range of turning point estimates is now significantly higher than original estimates.** Although some of the original studies had turning points in the $3,000 to $5,000 range, a number of studies have predicted much higher turning points. Many studies have found turning points such as $14,730 and $22,675 for sulfur, $9,800 for particulate matter, and $35,000 for carbon dioxide (Kaufman et al. 1998; Seldon and Song 1994; List and Gallet 1999). In some cases, a second wave of environmental degradation occurred at higher levels of income. Grossman and Krueger (1993) found that at income levels between $10,000 and $15,000 that levels of environmental degradation began to increase again. These studies indicate that environmental degradation could occur for decades before turning around—if it ever does.

– **Other significant factors, aside from national income, are important drivers of environmental change.** Variables such as the degree of political freedom and democracy in a nation, population density, economic structure, and historical events (such as the oil price shocks of the 1970s) have been found to be significantly correlated with levels of environmental degradation, in addition to or more importantly than income. These findings imply that environmental degradation, if it does decline, will not decline automatically (Torras 1996; Unruh 1997).

– **The EKC has not been shown to apply in the relatively small number of studies using historical time series for individual countries.** Most EKC studies utilize cross-sectional (or panel data) to estimate an average curve. Vincent (1997) noted that such an approach may simply be reflecting a positive relationship between environmental degradation and national income in developing countries (citing those studies that do incorporate developing countries) and a negative relationship for developed countries, but not a single relationship that can be expected for developed and developing countries alike. When estimating the historical experience of Malaysia, Vincent found no evidence of an inverted-U shaped curve for the six air and water pollutants he examined.

In addition to the limited empirical evidence, a number of authors cite other concerns while cautioning policy-makers against generalizing policy prescriptions from the EKC. One concern is the distinction between mean *vs.* median income. Early EKC's implied that environmental degradation would peak at mean world income. Given the fact that many countries were within reach of the mean, it was implied that environmental degradation may soon be on the decline (World Bank 1992). The global income distribution is quite skewed, however, with many more people below than above the mean. Using the median rather than the mean of global income would imply environmental degradation far into the future. Another concern is that the developed countries may have experienced EKCs partly because they now import pollution-intensive goods from less developed countries. It has been argued that many developing nations, such as China, will not have such a luxury (Lucas 1992; Suri 1998). Perhaps the major concern is that the environmental damage that occurs during the initial stages of economic development, prior to reaching any turning point, can be irreversible. Examples are deforestation (especially in old-growth forests), loss of biological and genetic diversity, loss of potable water, and deaths related to air pollution (Barbier 1994; Stern 1998). Finally, many have argued that extrapolating policy advice based on a cross-section of mostly developed countries to developing countries is problematic. Such an approach assumes that the development path of developed countries is easily replicable for the developing countries (Moomah and Unruh, 1997).

Environmental Kuznets Curve for Mexico?

According to the early EKC literature, and to the rhetoric of free trade proponents, by 1985 environmental degradation should have been on the decline in Mexico. In 1985, Mexico stood at a per capita level of income of roughly $5,000, beyond the point where early turning points were originally predicted to occur. Interestingly, 1985 is the same year Mexico began to rigorously integrate its economy with the United States and the world economy.

A National Institute for Statistics, Geography, and Informatics (INEGI) report, titled *Sistema de Cuentas Económicas y Ecológicas de Mexico,* includes national levels of data on a variety of environmental media and attempts to estimate the economic costs of such environmental degradation. This chapter uses that data to examine levels of environmental degradation from 1985 to 1999.

Despite the fact that Mexico reached levels of income beyond the range of a predicted EKC turning point, many environmental problems continue to worsen in Mexico. Figure 2.2 shows trends (expressed in physical quantities of pollution) for national levels of soil erosion, municipal solid waste, and urban air and water pollution from 1985 to 1999. According to these data, rural soil erosion grew by 89 percent, municipal solid waste by 108 percent, water pollution by 29 percent, and urban air pollution by 97 percent. These air pollution figures are national estimates of carbon monoxide (CO), nitrogen oxide (NO_x), sulfur oxide (SO_x), hydrocarbons (HC), and particulate matter (PT). Although Mexico City has witnessed a decrease in CO_2 and lead (Pb), there have been significant increases in other areas of Mexico, thus

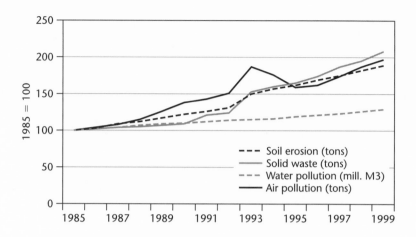

FIGURE **2.2** **Environmental Trends**

SOURCE: INEGI (2000), Sistema de Cuentas Ecónomicas y Ecológicas de Mexico.

"national" levels in these figures are increasing. In addition, these figures do not include Pb. However, PT, NO_x and SO_x comprise the main pollutants that the EKC was founded on. These specific pollutants are discussed in the following pages. Chapter 5 discusses air pollution in Mexico City (and in other parts of Mexico) in greater detail.

For these pollutants, there is no sign of a turning point for Mexico. These results are not surprising. The academic literature noted above would lead us to suspect that trends in solid waste, soil erosion, and water pollution would still be increasing in Mexico. The broader literature described above has found that evidence for an inverted-U shaped relationship has been limited to localized air pollutants. Figure 2.3 shows the relationship between SO_x in Mexico and GDP per capita. A number of simple regressions were carried out where tons of pollution per capita are regressed on GDP per capita and its square. For SO_x, NO_x, and PT, in addition to soil erosion, solid waste, and water pollution, there is no sign of an inverted-U relationship. These regressions suggest that the relationship between criteria air pollutants and income in Mexico is indeed parabolic, but that the parabola is going in the wrong direction than the EKC would lead one to expect—ever increasing pollution. Although the trend is not as sharply increasing as with the other pollutants, these air

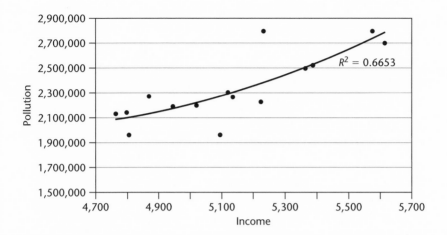

FIGURE **2.3**   EKC for SO$_x$?

pollutants have significantly increased during this period, ranging from 42 percent terms in the case of sulfur, to as high as 65 percent for NO$_x$.

These findings lend support to the broader literature on the EKC, particularly the literature as it pertains to developing countries. This analysis supports the idea that the results from cross-sectional developed country samples are difficult to generalize for developing countries. These findings, which utilize historical time series for an individual developing country, imply that if there will be an EKC turning point for Mexico, it will come further into the future than many would predict.

An additional finding runs counter to much of the academic literature, and to the intuition regarding developed country experiences: the case of CO$_2$. Figure 2.4 shows EKC regressions for CO$_2$ in Mexico from 1970 to 2000. This data comes from the Oak Ridge National Laboratory's Carbon Dioxide Information Analysis Center. As with the other pollutants discussed above, CO$_2$ emissions are outpacing income growth. From 1970 to 2000, CO$_2$ emissions (measured in thousands of metric tons) increased by 277 percent while real incomes only rose by 58 percent. During the period of economic integration examined in this study (1985 to 1999) emissions increased by 39 percent, while incomes grew by 12 percent. What is different for CO$_2$ is that emissions are increasing at a declining rate, indicating that Mexico could hit a turning point for

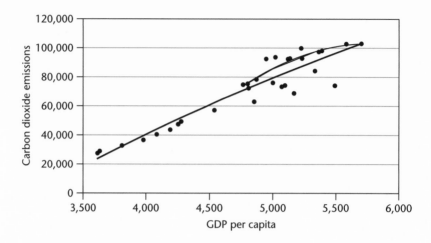

FIGURE **2.4**   EKC for CO$_2$?

carbon dioxide sooner than the pollutants described above (that are rising at an increasing rate).

Figure 2.4 exhibits the results of two different regressions of a carbon dioxide EKC for Mexico. One trend line shows the trend from 1970 to 1999. The upper line shows the trend from 1985 to 1999. The two regressions have adjusted r-squares at .86 and .71 respectively. Both trend lines show increases at a decreasing rate, but the trend is more defined during the 1985 to 1999 period.

Based on these trends it is possible to forecast the future value of the turning point for CO$_2$. If CO$_2$ emissions and GDP per capita bore the 1970 to 1999 relationship, Mexico would see a turning point at \$10,565 GDP per capita. At current GDP growth rates, it would take over 60 years to reach that point. Forecasting from the 1985 to 1999 trend, the turning point would be \$5,775, and would be reached in less than a decade at current growth rates. One explanation for why Mexico may be experiencing an EKC-like relationship for CO$_2$ is the fact that Mexico is extraordinarily rich in oil reserves. Referring back to table 2.4, note that emissions began to increase, yet at a decreasing rate beginning in 1985. 1985 marked the beginning of a major oil price drop. Since then, Mexico has been producing less oil as a percentage of GDP and is thus emitting less CO$_2$ in those terms.

The Economic Costs of Environmental Degradation

Environmental degradation has come at great cost to the Mexican economy. INEGI estimates that the economic costs of environmental degradation in Mexico were 10 percent of annual GDP from 1985 to 1999, or an average of $36 billion of damage each year ($47 billion for 1999). These costs overwhelm the value of economic growth, which has been just 2.6 percent annually over the same period, or $9 billion per year.

In this study mentioned above (INEGI 2000), INEGI calculated the economic costs of environmental degradation in Mexico in three different ways to capture the costs of numerous kinds of environmental damage. INEGI drew on net rent and user cost methodologies to estimate the value of lost natural resources such as deforestation, soil erosion, and so forth. The net rent method is a depreciation adjustment that was pioneered by the World Resources Institute. It subtracts annual changes in the market value of proven reserves of natural resources from gross investment on an annual basis (Repetto 1989). For other natural resources, the user cost, or the portion of receipts from selling a resource (net of extraction costs) that must be reinvested in order to maintain income after a natural resource has been depleted, are subtracted (Serafy 1993). INEGI used abatement cost estimates to determine the costs of environmental contamination. Based on information from Mexico's environmental agencies, INEGI's environmental damage cost estimate reflected the amount of funds required to reduce contamination levels to meet current standards.

Many international agencies now calculate estimates of the economic costs of environmental regulation. Using similar methods, the World Bank estimated that the economic costs of air and water pollution (a much narrower list of pollutants than used in the Mexico study) were 8 percent of China's GDP in 1995 (World Bank 1997). A study that examined a larger number of environmental problems in China estimated that the environmental costs of economic growth in China amounted to 13 percent of China's GDP (Smil 1998).

Degradation (or contamination) costs far outweigh natural resource costs in the INEGI calculations. The average annual economic costs of environmental contamination in Mexico from 1985 to 1999 were

9 percent of total GDP for contamination such as air and water pollution, and one percent for natural resource depletion. Of the various kinds of environmental contamination in Mexico, air pollution (the subject of the next three chapters) is the most costly. In 1985, air pollution represented 77 percent of the economic costs of environmental contamination in Mexico, by 1999 air pollution was 85 percent (or $39 billion of damage).

Estimating the Costs of Future Environmental Degradation

The analysis conducted in this chapter does not prove the EKC wrong. Consistent with the peer-reviewed literature on the subject, it may just be that the predicted turning points are further into the future. Theodore Panayatou (2001) has suggested that since it may take decades for a low-income country to cross from the upward to the downward sloping part of the curve, the accumulated damages in the meanwhile may far exceed the present value of high future growth. Therefore, active environmental policy to mitigate emissions and resource depletion in the early stages of development may be justified on purely economic grounds.

This section of the chapter estimates the economic cost of future environmental degradation under a business-as-usual scenario. Without the proper environmental policies in place, Mexico could experience costly levels of environmental degradation for over a century.

Guided by the EKC literature, Mexico's actual environmental trends from 1985 to 1999, in addition to the environmental damage cost estimates in INEGI's national accounts reports, it is possible to predict the economic costs of future environmental damage. There is a consensus that an EKC relationship has been found for criteria air pollutants, at least in the developed countries. The turning point when environmental degradation starts to decrease may be higher than $5,000 GDP per capita (Stern, 1998). This chapter then, rather than invalidating the EKC hypothesis for Mexico, simply shows that the turning point comes much further into the future.

Waiting for the prospect of an automatic environmental turn-around as predicted by the EKC would be very costly and damaging for Mexico. The results of the exercises (described in the appendix) for air pollution are presented in Table 2.1. At current rates of growth it would

TABLE **2.1**   Environmental Damage Costs at Various EKC Turning Points

		Damage Costs to Turning Point ($US billions)	
GDP per capita	Turning Point Year	(r = .06)	(r = .03)
$7,500	2028	79	114
$10,000	2057	105	194
$15,000	2097	119	279

SOURCE: GDP per capita figures adapted from World Bank Development Indicators, Damage Cost Estimates derived from INEGI.

take Mexico 30 years to reach a turning point for criteria air pollutants of $7,500 of income, and 99 years to reach the turning point of $15,000. The costs of the damage that would occur until Mexico reached the turning point could be as high as $279 billion, more than half of Mexico's total output in 2001.

Assuming that the EKC relationship is parabolic, it would take twice as long for Mexico to return to the already high and costly 1998 levels of criteria air pollution. If Mexico experiences an EKC turning point of $7,500 GDP per capita for criteria air pollutants, it would not be until 2058 before Mexico returned to the already high levels of air pollution that occurred in 1998. If the turning point was $15,000, Mexico would not return to 1998 levels until 2197, and could cost as much as $300 billion in today's terms. These values are more than half the current value of Mexico's GDP.

Summary and Conclusions

Mexico has not yet been able to tame the environmental impacts of economic growth. The effects of these shortcomings have been very costly to the Mexican economy, and the costs of inadequate attention to the environment promise to escalate far into the future.

They key findings in this chapter are:

– There is no sign of an inverted-U relationship between economic growth and environmental degradation for the majority of pollutants in Mexico examined in this chapter. If there is an EKC for Mexico, the turning point must be well above current income levels.

- CO_2 emissions may be experiencing an EKC-like pattern. Based on recent trends, it could take between 10 and 60 years to reach a turning point for this pollutant.
- The economic costs of environmental degradation in Mexico have been very significant. From 1985 to 1999, such costs have averaged 10 percent of annual GDP, or $36 billion dollars per year. This trend stands in stark contrast to economic growth during that period, which only stood at 2.6 percent annually, or $9 billion per year. Air pollution is the most costly form of contamination in Mexico, representing 87 percent of the costs of environmental contamination.
- Without a dramatic change in Mexican environmental policy, Mexico's environmental degradation will increase significantly into the future. If there is an EKC with a higher turning point, business as usual scenarios estimate that Mexico may "turn around" in 30 years, but cost over $100 billion in today's terms. Other plausible estimates show that it may be closer to 100 years.

The following four chapters examine the factors that are causing increasing environmental degradation in Mexico.

3   Is Mexico a Pollution Haven?

During the hotly contested debates over passage of the North American Free Trade Agreement (NAFTA), environmentalists' biggest fear was that Mexico would become a pollution haven for U.S. companies. Such fears were far from alleviated by economic theory, nor by the environmental record of Mexico's maquiladora program. Now there are ample data to look at Mexico's period of economic integration and ask the question: Is Mexico a pollution haven?

The answer is: no. The analysis in this chapter shows that the marginal costs of pollution abatement are such a relatively small expense that they are not major factors when the majority of firms are making decisions regarding their location. This result has important implications for public policy. A number of actors in both the United States and Mexico often claim that the costs of environmental protection will curtail the ability of businesses to be competitive. Based on these claims, they argue against building the capacity of government to respond to the environmental consequences of economic integration. Such arguments are unjustified. Creating optimal environmental policies in both countries could bring higher economic welfare to each party.

This chapter is divided into three parts: 1) discussion of the empirical evidence regarding pollution havens, particularly of previous studies of pollution haven effects in Mexico, 2) presentation of the results of a regression analysis (as described in the appendix), and 3) presentation of conclusions and policy considerations.

Empirical Evidence for the Pollution Haven Hypothesis

As discussed in Chapter 1, economic theory implies that the liberalization of trade between two countries with different levels of environmental protection could lead pollution-intensive industry to concentrate in the nation where environmental regulation is most lax (or less costly). Such logic forms the basis of the pollution haven hypothesis.

Such logic has been extended into the regulatory sphere as well. It has been argued that the fear of losing comparative advantage because of increasing marginal pollution costs would cause a race to the bottom in environmental regulation. Not only would firms flock to areas where pollution control costs are relatively less costly, firms would also exert downward pressure on environmental standards in nations with more optimal environmental policies, all in the name of competition (Esty 1999; Neumayer 2001). From the perspective of the country that lacks optimal environmental policies, there are concerns that such countries could be stuck at the bottom. This result could occur because nations might fear that increasing levels of environmental protections (and therefore costs) would scare away foreign investment. Nations with differing levels of environmental policy face a classic prisoner's dilemma: competitive pressures give individual countries the incentive to pursue lower environmental policy than if they worked collectively, although cooperation between the countries would result in greater welfare for all countries (Zarsky 1997; see also Porter 1999).

There is very limited empirical support for the pollution haven hypothesis. The bulk of the large and growing body of empirical literature testing for pollution havens in the global economy has found no observable sign of a pollution haven. The vast majority of studies have found no systematic evidence that the share of developing country exports and production is becoming more pollution-intensive. In addition, no studies have indicated that there is substantial evidence that pollution-intensive industries flee developed countries with relatively high (and costly) environmental standards (for comprehensive reviews of this empirical work see Jaffe 1995; Jayadevappa 2000; Panayotou 2000; Neumayer 2001).

In the highly politicized NAFTA debates, at least anecdotally, Mexico was a different case. The U.S.-Mexico border region's maquiladora plants were generally seen as an environmental disaster, California-based furniture makers had reportedly moved to Mexico to avoid installing air pollution fixtures, Mexico's officials were said to have made statements attempting to lure U.S. firms by making low regulatory compliance costs part of their sales pitch. These were all pointed to as evidence of pollution havens in Mexico that would be exacerbated under NAFTA (Mayer 1998).

Interestingly, only a handful of economists have attempted to empirically test whether the evidence of pollution havens in Mexico has become widespread. Those studies that have been conducted are largely consistent with the peer-reviewed literature: these studies find no evidence in support of the pollution-haven hypothesis. Grossman and Krueger (1993) performed the only such study during the NAFTA debates. In a cross-industry comparison of data in one year, 1987, the authors tested whether pollution abatement costs in U.S. industries affected imports from Mexico, as one would expect if Mexico was functioning as a pollution haven relative to the United States. They found the impact of cross-industry differences in pollution abatement costs on U.S. imports from Mexico to be positive, but small and statistically insignificant. Traditional economic determinants of trade and investment, such as factor prices and tariffs, were found to be far more significant.

A more recent study examined whether pollution abatement costs affected patterns of U.S. foreign investment into Mexico and three other countries. Also a cross-industry comparison of data in one year, this time 1990, this study had similar results to those of Grossman and Krueger. The authors did find a positive relationship between pollution abatement costs and levels of Foreign Direct Investment (FDI). Such a relationship was not found to be statistically significant (Eskeland and Harrison 1997). Kahn (2000) is the only study to examine this question over time. Rather than looking at the costs of pollution abatement like the previous two studies, Kahn looked at the pollution intensity (using U.S. Toxic Release Inventory Data) of U.S. trade with Mexico and other countries in 1972, 1982, and 1992. He found the pollution content of U.S. imports from Mexico had slightly declined during the period (Kahn 2001).

Although these studies are commendable, they do suffer from a number of limitations. Perhaps the most important limitation is the lack of attention to the effect of marginal environmental costs in the United States on Mexican economic activity during the full time period of economic integration in Mexico. The first two studies cited above that looked at Mexico were snapshot cross-industry comparisons in one year. The third study mentioned, by Kahn, does look at Mexican economic activity over time but does not look at costs, and does not examine the post-NAFTA period. This chapter addresses some of these concerns.

Is Mexico a Pollution Haven?

After performing a fairly extensive set of regressions that improve on previous work and that are described in the appendix, this chapter fails to find Mexico to be a pollution haven for the majority of highly polluting U.S. companies. Such findings are consistent with previous studies on pollution havens in Mexico, and with the broader literature on the pollution haven hypothesis as a whole.

An examination of the raw data foreshadows the regression results. Table 3.1 exhibits the shares of production and employment in the five dirtiest U.S. industries (discussed in the previous section as measured by pollution abatement costs) to total industrial production and employment. These shares are calculated for both the United States and Mexico for 1988, 1994, and 1998. The dirty industry share of production in the United States did slightly decline over this period, but declined in Mexico—and even faster. The United States is also not losing jobs to

TABLE **3.1** No Migration of Top Five "Dirty" Industries to Mexico

	1988	1994	1998
Mexico			
production	30.1%	23.1%	26.5%
employment	7.9%	6.3%	5.9%
US			
production	17.0%	15.1%	14.7%
employment	11.3%	11.2%	11.2%

SOURCE: Author's calculations based on UNIDO (2000).

dirty production in Mexico. Employment in dirty industries in the United States has remained the same, and has actually declined in Mexico.

Regression analysis allows the analyst to feel more secure about the relationships exhibited in the raw data. If Mexico has become a pollution haven for U.S. industries looking to flee the costs of pollution abatement in the United States, we would expect that an analysis that involved regressing the effect of the costs of pollution on location decisions in Mexico would result in the pollution variables would be positive and statistically significant. If the abatement cost variable is positive and statistically significant, that indicates that Mexican output expanded more as the amount of pollution abatement increased in corresponding industries in the U.S. In other words, as predicted by the Heckscher-Ohlin theory discussed in Chapter 1, industry locates where it is less costly to abate pollution. We would expect the same result when the economic variables are regressed on the ratio of Mexico to U.S. pollution intensity as well. In this case, if the pollution coefficient is positive and statistically significant, output would expand more in Mexico in those industries that are dirtier in Mexico than in their U.S. counterparts.

To conduct this analysis, 12 different regressions were performed (see Appendix for details). The results are presented in Table 3.2. Six

TABLE **3.2**   Regression Results

Dependent Variables	Model 1 Independent Variable: Abatement Costs			Model 2 Independent Variable: Mexico-US intensity ratio		
	β	p values	adj R^2	β	p values	adj R^2
84–99						
Growth in Mexican Exports	0.679	0.387	−0.01	−0.00007	0.303	0.0052
Growth Mexican Production	−0.119	0.792	−0.04	−0.00005	0.139	0.0586
Growth in Mexican Export Share of US Consumption	0.399	0.648	−0.04	−0.00004	0.496	−0.0243
post-NAFTA						
Growth in Mexican Exports	−3.82	0.577	−0.03	−0.003	0.637	−0.0363
Growth Mexican Production	−1.204	0.401	−0.01	0.00006	0.603	−0.0339
Growth in Mexican Export Share of US Consumption	−3.845	0.548	−0.03	−0.0003	0.592	−0.0331
N	27			27		

SOURCE: Author's regression analyses (see appendix).

different dependent variables are listed in the first column. The two independent variables, each of which is run in separate bi-variate regressions with each of the dependent variables, form the next two columns. The independent variables are labeled Model 1, and Model 2. In Model 1, each dependent variable is regressed on marginal abatement costs in the U.S. This pollution variable is the sum of all of the marginal abatement costs for each pollutant for an entire industry. In Model 2, each dependent variable is regressed on the ratio of air pollution intensity in Mexico to air pollution intensity in the United States. The estimated coefficients, p-values, and adjusted R-square are found in corresponding rows.

None are significant, and 9 of the 12 coefficients have the wrong sign. With the Model 1 regressions, for dependent variables during the full period of economic integration in Mexico, 1984 to 1999, the coefficients for Mexican exports and production are positive. This indicates that output expanded in Mexican industries where pollution is most costly to abate in the United States. As was the case with previous studies by Grossman and Krueger and Eskelund and Harrison, these numbers are small and statistically insignificant. The sign changes when analyzing dependent variables in the post-NAFTA period. After NAFTA was passed, those industries where pollution was most costly to abate in the United States actually grew at a slower rate in Mexico. In each case, the magnitude of such change was small and statistically insignificant.

Model 2 results are presented in the second column. The dependent variables of economic activity in Mexico are regressed on the ratio of air pollution emissions intensity in Mexico to air pollution emissions intensity in the United States. If Mexico became a pollution haven, production in Mexico would be expanding faster in those Mexican industries where it was possible to pollute more than a firm could in the United States. Separate regressions were performed—using ratios for sulfur oxides (SO_x), nitrous oxides (NO_x), and particulate matter (PT), and for all ratios averaged across all three pollutants. Air pollution emissions per unit of output for all pollutants were averaged for each industry to create one measure of air pollution emissions intensity for each industry. The results were broadly similar for all variants of Model 2 (single pollutant and multiple pollutant ratios); the multiple pollutant ratio results are presented in Table 4.3. From 1984 to 1999, and in the post-NAFTA period, on average, in those industries that were relatively more air pollution emissions intensive in Mexico, economic activity in Mexico decreased. As the Model 2 coefficients in Table 4.3 indicate, such changes were truly miniscule, and all of them were statistically insignificant.

Analysis and Conclusions

Consistent with the academic literature on the subject, the numerous tests conducted in this chapter all failed to support the pollution haven hypothesis for Mexico. High pollution abatement costs in the United States are not significantly correlated to the levels of economic activity in Mexico during the period of economic integration (1984 to 1998) or to the changes in economic activity since NAFTA.

The reason why this result consistently appears in this study and others like it is quite simple: even at the margin, the costs of pollution are too small to significantly factor into the average firm's location decisions. A related explanation is that many firms are simply too large and cumbersome to move to another location, and they need to stay close to their product markets. The marginal abatement costs are small related to the transaction costs of decommissioning and actually moving to another country (Neumayer 2001).

Although this study is consistent with similar studies for Mexico, all of this work to date suffers from two data and measurement issues that may be skewing the results. First, the empirical examinations of pollution havens for Mexico all look at very aggregated levels of data for economic activity. Most studies look at 2-digit, 3-digit (such as this one), and 4-digit industries in the economies examined. Such examinations can inform us that there are no widespread pollution havens, but it does not say that pollution havens do not exist at all. In fact, we know there are leaders and laggards with respect to environmental standards among U.S. companies doing business in Mexico. To take the electricity industry as an example, a plant in Mexico being built by InterGen (owned by Shell Oil and Bechtel), will not comply to U.S. standards even though the electricity will be serving the U.S. market. On the other hand, a similar electricity plant is being built in Mexico by Sempra Energy Group Enterprises, but that plant will adhere to California's stringent environmental standards. A representative from Sempra has said "we thought it was good business and it made environmental sense" (Weiner 2002). Such leaders and laggards cannot be picked up in the aggregate level analyses conducted in this and the other examinations of the pollution haven hypothesis for Mexico.

A second set of data-related problems are perhaps even more grave. When conducting studies such as these, the marginal pollution abatement costs (or levels of pollution) for individual industries are estimates. As has been shown in Mexico, the environmental problems that occur within the firm's grounds can be less severe than pollution problems in the surrounding community that arise as a result of internal migration by employees to work at the firms themselves. Mexico's notable maquiladora environmental problems are the lack of sewage treatment facilities, the lack of adequate roads and other infrastructure (which exacerbate air and water pollution problems), and an increase in inefficient automobile and trucking transportation (OECD 1997). While problems such as plant-level air and water pollution, and the handling of toxic pollutants on the job certainly persist in maquiladoras, these community environmental problems are those in most crisis. Such problems are seen as a function of internal migration to work at the plants in question. Local municipalities desperate for investment lack the ability to erect the necessary fiscal measures to provide basic services to these rapidly swelling populations. The author's calculations do not pick up such effects.

Case study research is needed to identify the leaders and laggards among U.S. corporations in Mexico. Following this discussion, special attention should be paid to the extent to which U.S. firms adhere to environmental standards within the plant grounds. Just as important, however, is the degree to which these firms enable their host communities to alleviate the pressing environmental problems that occur as a result of massive internal migration to the areas where U.S. firms locate.

Using the best available data to date, the results of this chapter show that there was no widespread race to the bottom of dirty industries fleeing the United States to Mexico. These results have important implications for public policy. The U.S. business community often argues against environmental regulations in the name of competitiveness. Developing countries such as Mexico are said to be wary of developing optimal environmental policies for fear of scaring away investment (Zarsky 1997). What these results show is that there is plenty of room to elevate environmental standards in both countries. The costs of abating pollution in the United States will not make firms leave the country: the costs of abating pollution in Mexico will not deter firms from investing in Mexico.

Chapter 1 has shown that environmental degradation is increasing in Mexico. Contrary to what many predicted, this trend is not a result of Mexico becoming a pollution haven for U.S. companies. Economic integration can cause scale, composition, and technology effects of pollution that are independent of pollution effects of the Hecksher-Ohlin type that are analyzed in this chapter. The next two chapters form a case study of industrial air pollution in Mexico that examines the degree to which these three effects are causing increased environmental degradation in Mexico.

4   A Change in Composition: The Case of Industrial Air Pollution I

In a little over a decade, Mexico has transformed itself from an import substituting, oil exporting economy, to an integrated economy with manufactures as its chief export. Also during that time, environmental problems grew faster than the economy. Air pollution has been identified as one of the most severe and costly of environmental problems in Mexico. Yet, such environmental problems are not a function of Mexico serving as a pollution haven for dirty U.S. firms. What then, is causing the increasing environmental degradation?

This chapter (and the chapter that follows) serves as a case study that attempts to provide the answer to that question. The scale, composition, and technique effects of criteria air pollution are analyzed for Mexican manufacturing during the period 1985 to 1999. The scale and composition effects of criteria air pollutants in Mexican manufacturing are also calculated. These analyses are followed by two counterfactual analyses that ask two questions: What if the reform policies had not gone into effect? and Did the structural or compositional changes that resulted from Mexico's transition from a relatively closed to an open economy lead to a concentration of more or less criteria-air pollution intensive industry?

Mexican manufacturing is now relatively less pollution intensive. Manufacturing growth overall has been fairly impressive, therefore total pollution (or the scale effect) continues to increase. Economic integration did not cause compositional shifts that automatically improved the criteria air pollution in industry.

This chapter consists of four parts: 1) a brief overview of criteria air pollution in Mexico; 2) a short review of past studies on industrial pollution in Mexico; 3) an analysis of the scale and composition effects of criteria air pollution in Mexican manufacturing; and 4) conclusions and suggestions for further research. The appendix includes a discussion of the data and methodologies employed in this chapter.

Criteria Air Pollution in Mexico

Air pollution ranks among the most acute environmental problems in Mexico. Although the bulk of air pollution in Mexico comes from mobile sources, industrial air emissions are also significant. The impact of industrial emissions is often overlooked.

It should not be a surprise that Mexican air pollution has grown at a rapid pace. Mexico City has long been recognized as one of the world's most polluted cities. In 1998, Mexico City ranked fifth in the world for total emissions of particulate matter (PT), tenth in sulfur dioxide (SO_2), and second in nitrogen oxides (NO_x). However, in some cases air pollution in Mexico City has improved significantly. Ambient concentrations of SO_2, lead (Pb), and NO_x all decreased significantly during the 1990s. Such reductions have been attributed to: the introduction of catalytic converters in new gasoline vehicles, tightening of gasoline emissions standards, the introduction of unleaded gasoline (and a parallel lead phase-out), and other programs (Molina 2002).

Ozone (O_3) and PT concentrations however, are still very acute in Mexico City. Ozone standards are still in violation for more than 80 percent of the year in Mexico, compared to 13 percent for Los Angeles (Molina 2002). Between 1988 and 1998, annual ambient concentrations of O_3 in Mexico City increased by 44 percent (Semarnap 2000). PT standards are still in violation for close to 40 percent of the year in Mexico City (Molina 2002).

Exposure to PT and O_3 have had the most severe effects on human health among air pollutants in Mexico (Margulis 1996). A consistent finding among those examining the health effects of air pollution in Mexico City is that for each 1 ug/m^3 increase in levels of particulate matter, mortality rates increase by 1.3 percent (Molina 2002). Health effects also include chronic bronchitis, loss of work days, and respiratory problems that result in restricted activity days. The U.S. Environmental Protection Agency (EPA) has estimated the economic value of these health effects in the United States to be just short of $5 million dollars per statistical life (summing the mortality costs per statistical life, bronchitis cases, loss of work days, and restricted days). Extrapolating from these figures, Mexican researchers estimate that figure to be a little less than $2 million per life (Molina 2002).

More recently, industrial centers outside Mexico City have experienced unprecedented growth in economic activity and population. These centers, such as Monterrey, Guadalajara, and the border region, are fast becoming highly polluted as well. For example, air pollution standards are now exceeded 90 percent of the year in Guadalajara (DOE 2002). On a national level, average urban criteria air pollutants hydrocarbons (HC), PT, CO, SO_2 and NO_x) grew by 97 percent between 1985 and 1999, or 5 percent on an annual basis. The Mexican economy only grew by 38 percent during that time, or 2.6 percent annually.

The high degree of criteria air pollution in Mexico's metropolitan areas come from vehicle emissions. Vehicular emissions have thus been the focus of the majority of attention in both scholarly and policy circles. What receives less attention are industrial emissions.

What is not often pointed out is that industry is an important contributor to levels of air pollution in Mexico as well. Table 4.1 shows that on a national level, such emissions are significant for PT, SO_2, and NO_x (CO and HC are primarily from motor vehicles, although the electronics

TABLE **4.1**   Industrial Air Pollution as a Share of Total Air Pollution in Four
Mexican Cities

	PT	SO_2	CO	NO_x	HC
National Average	20%	22%	0.07%	17%	0.04%
Guadalajara	21%	68%	0.15%	8%	3%
Monterrey	89%	92%	0.36%	35%	4%
Toluca	34%	82%	0.08%	10%	7%
Mexico City	41%	64%	0.39%	24%	3%

SOURCE: Estadisticas del Medio Ambiente, Mexico 1999 (Tomo II) Mexicali Inventory Group Binational Advisory Committee.

and automobile industries do emit noticeable amounts of HC). Manufacturing emissions for PT, SO_2, and NO_x occur because the industrial sector is a relatively large consumer of energy, and in some cases uses particularly air pollution intensive fuels. NO_x and HC together cause the secondary formation of O_3. Sulfur Oxides (SO_x) also contribute to the secondary formation of PT (Vijay 2001). Table 4.1 also shows that in Mexico's industrial regions, industrial emissions are much higher than the national average (Toluca is a refining area).

How have such trends changed during Mexico's period of economic integration? The remaining portion of this chapter will examine this question based on a theoretical framework first developed by Grossman and Krueger (1993) who have shown how growth from economic integration can affect the environment in three ways: scale, composition, and technique effects.[1]

Industrial Pollution in Mexico: Review of Previous Studies

A handful of studies have attempted to estimate the scale and composition effects on industrial pollution in Mexico. These studies have shed a great deal of light on the relationship between economic growth and the environment in Mexico, but have suffered from two limitations that pertain to the data used for analysis. First, many of the earlier studies were forced to rely on estimates of 1987 levels of pollution in the United States as proxies for Mexico. Second, although an important series of Mexico-specific coefficients was released in 1997, the data has been found to have a number of shortcomings.

The Industrial Pollution Projection System

During the late 1980s, the World Bank produced an invaluable set of tools to help economists examine levels of environmental degradation in developing countries, the Industrial Pollution Projection System (IPPS). The IPPS was created "to exploit the fact that industrial pollution is

---

1. OECD (1994) adds a fourth effect, a regulatory effect whereby trade laws directly affect national environmental regulations. Regulatory effects will not be of focus in this chapter.

heavily affected by the scale of industrial activity and its sectoral composition" (Hettige, Martin et al. 1994, 2). The IPPS is a system of pollution coefficients (or intensities) for air, soil, and water pollution based on levels in the United States in 1987. These intensities are presented in terms of pollution per unit of output or per employee for various branches of industry. These data have been used as a proxy for industrial pollution in a number of developing countries such as Brazil, Latvia, India, and Vietnam.

IPPS coefficients have been used in a few studies to analyze industrial pollution in Mexico. Ten Kate (1993) was the first to apply the IPPS to Mexico. He found that pollution due to the composition effect within the Mexican manufacturing sector increased by approximately 50 percent between 1950 and 1970, and by 25 percent from 1970 until 1989. Ten Kate also found that manufactures were producing 20 times as much total pollution in 1989 as in 1950, implying that most of the growth in emissions is from the scale effect (Ten Kate 1993). A more recent study looked at the pollution intensity of Mexican exports in the pre- and post-NAFTA period. That study found that there was a composition shift in Mexican exports toward less polluting sectors. However, the same study found a significant scale effect that outweighed such compositional changes (Schatan 2002).

Air Pollution Intensities for Mexico

In recognition of the need to create developing country-specific pollution measures, during the late 1990s, the World Bank created a series of air pollution intensities for Mexico and China. Although these data are a major improvement over the IPPS coefficients, the new Mexico data suffers from a variety of limitations. With colleagues from the Mexican government and an academic research institute in Mexico, the author outlined these shortfalls and presented a corrected set of data.

For the Mexico data, the World Bank obtained air pollution data from Mexico's National Institute of Ecology (INE). As part of Mexico's national environmental policy, a number of the key Mexican industries are required to report air emissions. These emissions are reported when new firms submit mandatory environmental impact statements, and in the form of annual reports called Cedula de Operation Annual (COA).

These data are fed into the National System of Information for Fixed Sources (SNIFF), the database used by the World Bank.

SNIFF contains emissions data for five criteria air pollutants: NO_x, SO_x, PT, CO, and HC. In addition to emissions, it also contains data on energy consumption, energy technology, smokestacks, and basic economic data for each firm. The emissions data is collected in two forms. For some firms, especially those who are mandated to report to COA, emissions are reported from monitoring systems directly at each facility. For the majority of firms, however, emissions are calculated algebraically using the AP-42 method created by the U.S. EPA. The latter approach creates engineering based "emissions factors" that are estimated based on a firm's energy use, production process, pollution control equipment, and inputs (INE 1996; INE/SEMARNAP 1999).

With SNIFF data, the World Bank created air pollution intensities in the form of pollution per employee (at the two- and three-digit Industrial Standard Industrial Classification (ISIC) levels) coefficients for 28 manufacturing industries. Published in 1997, these intensities represent Mexican industry during the 1993 to 1995 period. The World Bank coefficients were calculated for three firm sizes: small, medium, and large. One overall coefficient was also created to represent the industry as a whole. Small firms were defined as those with 20 or fewer employees, medium firms with employees between 21 and 100, and large ones with employment levels over 100. The distribution of the World Bank sample was 2,346 for small firms, 2,143 medium, and 1,310 for large. However, the World Bank reports that "preliminary analysis of results revealed an outlier problem. Therefore, the top 25 polluters were deleted from the overall dataset, and the top ten polluters from each plant-size category were removed, before calculation of pollution intensities"[2] (World Bank 2002). Because these plants were removed it is safe to assume that the data is biased downward.

Thus far, the intensities for Mexico have been used in only a few studies. Jenkins (1998) used these new data to examine the composition effect of Mexican manufactures from 1970 to 1988 (to compare with the Ten Kate results), and from 1988 to 1995. Where Ten Kate found a

2. When interviewed about the subject the World Bank was not sure why the most polluted firms were excluded and which firms were deleted from the dataset.

25 percent increase in the pollution intensity of Mexican manufacturing from 1970 to 1989 due to the composition effect, Jenkins, working with the new intensity data, found that the composition of pollution intensive industry in the Mexican economy remained relatively the same. During the period 1988 to 1995, Jenkins found an overall shift in composition away from pollution intensive industry. Mexican manufacturing by air pollution intensive industries fell in relation to less pollution intensive sectors (Jenkins 1998).

Limitations with Existing Research

There are two limitations to these past studies on the scale and composition effects of air pollution in Mexican industry. First, the United States-based IPPS data is not an adequate proxy for pollution in Mexico. Second, newer World Bank air pollution intensity data for Mexico has a number of shortcomings. The short discussion that follows here (and is expanded upon in the appendix), is a summary of a working paper that the author and others wrote on the subject of the World Bank intensities for Mexico. The World Bank welcomed our efforts. Indeed, they now offer the working paper and the corrected dataset on their web page.

Although the IPPS coefficients have been a great contribution to economic research, they do not perform well in the case of Mexico. As the World Bank country-specific intensity estimates reveal, there are large differences in emissions intensities between countries. Table 4.2 shows

TABLE **4.2** SO_x Intensity in U.S. Mexico and China

	U.S.	Mexico	China
Food and Beverages	0.50	1.71	15.89
Textiles and Apparel	0.35	1.56	11.50
Wood and Wood Products	0.36	0.68	43.04
Paper, Printing, and Publishing	2.33	5.67	26.63
Chemicals and Petroleum Products	3.16	2.80	84.52
Non-Metallic Mineral Products	6.19	1.96	44.38
Iron and Steel, Non-ferrous Metals	11.89	1.12	n.a.
Fabricated Metals and Machinery	0.15	0.08	4.30

SOURCE: Calculated from World Bank New Ideas and Pollution Regulation web page, www.worldbank.org/nipr.

comparable intensities for SO_x in China, Mexico, and the United States for manufactures (two-digit ISIC codes). This table reveals that not only were the U.S. intensities far from representative proxies of the magnitude of pollution levels in these two developing countries, they do not represent an ordinal representation of pollution intensity as well. On average, the Mexican intensities are twice that of the U.S. intensities, while the Chinese intensity for SO_x is 68 times that of the U.S. (Note that some Mexican industries are cleaner than their U.S. counterparts).

The World Bank intensities for Mexico are a marked improvement, but the new data still suffers from a number of shortcomings. The following description of these limitations is based on collaborative work the author conducted with colleagues at the Program for Science, Technology, and Development at El Colegio de Mexico, and at Mexico's National Institute of Ecology (INE). This work has been published as a working paper and is available on the World Bank's New Ideas in Pollution Regulation web page (Aguayo and Gallagher 2001). A shorter description of these data is offered as an appendix at the end of this article.

Whether in the case of the IPPS coefficients, or the newer coefficients for Mexico, data is available for only one year. For that reason, technology must be assumed to be fixed throughout the time period under examination. This is a serious limitation of all previous studies. Unfortunately, such an assumption must also be made in this study as well. This study will at least give the reader an idea of compositional changes in the post-NAFTA period. Such an analysis (conducted with data that is specific to Mexican manufacturing and not coefficients based on U.S. manufacturing) is also an improvement because it does not have to assume that levels of technology are the same in the United States and in Mexico.

A Change in Composition

Using the corrected intensities, the author calculated the scale and composition effects for air pollution in manufacturing. Calculations based on the equations outlined in the appendix reveal that despite compositional shifts toward relatively less criteria air pollution intensive industries in Mexico, during the period of economic integration, increases in the

TABLE **4.3**   Net Levels of Industrial Air Pollution,
1984 to 1998 (percent change)

	1984 to 1998	1984 to 1994	1994 to 1998
PT	18	−11	33
SO_x	8	−19	34
NO_x	23	−13	41

SOURCE: Author's calculations based on World Bank and
UNIDO data.

scale effect outweighed those compositional changes for manufacturing as a whole. For two of the three pollutants under examination in this chapter, total manufacturing emissions intensity is dirtier than oil refining.

Tables 4.3 and 4.4 present the changes in net levels of pollution (see equation 4 in the appendix) for all of Mexican manufacturing during the period 1984 to 1998. The period of intense economic integration in Mexico fell between 1987 to 1994, beginning with Mexico's accession to the General Agreement on Tariffs and Trade (GATT), and culminating with the NAFTA. Thus, starting with data for 1984, three years before integration got fully off the ground, and ending in 1998, four years after

TABLE **4.4**   Changes in Net Pollution, 1984 to 1998
(percent change)

	(1984 to 1998)	(1988 to 1998)
PT		
scale	23	17
composition	−301	−252
net	18	12
SO_x		
scale	23	17
composition	−119	−116
net	8	2
NO_x		
scale	23	17
composition	8	−54
net	23	12

SOURCE: Author's calculations based on World Bank and
UNIDO data.

TABLE **4.5**   8 Most Air Pollution-Intensive
Industries in Mexico

Pulp and Paper
Iron and Steel
Industrial Chemicals
Non-ferrous metals
Machinery
Non-metallic mineral products
Food Products
Beverage Products

SOURCE: Author's calculations based on World Bank
and UNIDO data.

NAFTA was passed, allows ample time for examination of the effects before and after economic integration.

Between 1984 and 1998, Table 4.3 shows that net PT emissions in Mexican manufacturing grew by 18 percent, SO_x by 8 percent, and NO_x by 23 percent. All levels in 1994, the year NAFTA went into force, are down due to the peso crisis when the dollar value was temporarily lowered by the exchange rate. For that reason, the changes since NAFTA are more pronounced: net levels of PT grew by 33 percent, SO_x by 34 percent, and NO_x by 41 percent.

Table 4.4 shows that there were compositional shifts away from more pollution intensive industries in Mexico for two of the three pollutants: PT and SO_x. This is due to the fact that, except for machinery, non-ferrous metals, and beverages sectors, the pollution intensive industries grew slower than manufacturing as a whole.

Based on the corrected World Bank air pollution intensities described in the previous section, Table 4.5 lists the eight most air pollution intensive industries in Mexico. Most are the same industries that appear on lists of the most air pollution intensive industries in the global economy (Mani 1999).[3] Air pollution is considered to be a function of either or both of the following: energy consumption waste or byproducts of the production process. Industries on the list for Mexico such as iron and steel products are those where pollution is more often a function of energy consumption. Industries like food and beverages, or industrial

---

3. Petroleum refining is not analyzed in this paper because Mexico does not consider it an industrial activity and therefore data is not included in the industrial census.

chemicals, are sometimes classified as those where pollution is a function of the production process. Most industries have parts of the production chain that entail both. The pulp and paper industry is a large energy consumer that can also emit large amounts of pollutants through the bleaching process (Bartzokas and Yarime 1997).

Table 4.5 exhibits the most criteria air pollution-intensive sectors in Mexico (ranked by taking the simple average of the pollution intensity of each pollutant). In addition to intensity, these industries are also the largest polluters in Mexico because they are among the largest sectors in Mexican manufacturing. Together, these 10 industries made up 50 percent of value added in Mexican industry. The coal products industry is quite a small industry in value added terms for Mexico, but it is still one of the biggest air polluters. In 1998, food, machinery, industrial chemicals and coal were among the biggest PT polluters and coal, iron and steel, non-ferrous metals, and pulp and paper were among the biggest SO_x and NO_x emitters.

Table 4.6 shows that the case of SO_x is the most pronounced. In this table, the results of the scale, composition, and net effects are shown for SO_x in the eight most pollution intensive industries, and the rest of manufacturing (see equations 2, 3, and 4). As shown in the second column, SO_x intensive industries such as the pulp and paper industry (the

TABLE **4.6** SO_x in Eight Dirtiest Industries, 1984 to 1998

	Scale	Composition (tons of SO_x)	Net
Pulp and Paper	3,635	−5,108	−1,473
Iron and Steel	3,107	−1,101	2,006
Industrial Chemicals	1,322	−1,198	124
Non-ferrous metals	782	1,005	1,787
Machinery	549	1,077	1,625
Non-metallic mineral products	704	−335	369
Food Products	4,828	−1,051	3,777
Beverage Products	3,208	−708	2,500
Subtotal	18,136	−7,420	10,716
Rest of Manufacturing	5,479	−6,733	−1,254
Total	23,614	−14,153	9,461

SOURCE: Author's calculations based on (UNIDO 2000; World Bank 2000).

most SO_x intensive), iron and steel, industrial chemicals, and food products grew much slower than manufacturing as a whole.

Two Counterfactual Analyses

Two interesting counterfactual questions may be asked with the calculations performed earlier in this chapter in hand. The first question is: If Mexico had continued to be primarily an oil exporting country (as it was before 1985) rather than a manufactures export economy, would Mexican exports be more or less air pollution intensive? That is, what if the changes in the 1980s had never happened? The second question is: If NAFTA had never happened, would the scale and composition of Mexican production be more or less air pollution intensive?

The first counterfactual involves dividing net levels of pollution in 1994 for all of manufactures by total production in the same year (in both cases net of oil emissions and production). This number represents the pollution intensity of the entire manufacturing sector in that year, and can then be compared to the pollution intensity coefficients for oil refining in the same year. If the coefficient for oil production is greater than the coefficient for manufacturing, assuming that oil exports would have grown at the same rate as manufactures then maintaining a path of oil exports (as opposed to economic integration) may have been more pollution-intensive than the current path.

When considering the levels of pollution in the export sector, it is common to consider the possibility that despite the growing amount of pollution in the export sector, it still amounts to less pollution than would have occurred if Mexico continued to rely on oil exports as its primary medium of foreign trade. To test this hypothesis, the author compared the pollution intensity of the Mexican manufacturing industry as a whole, with the intensity coefficient for the oil refining sector. The results are presented in Table 4.7.

In the case of NO_x, the counterfactual hypothesis that oil refining is much dirtier than manufacturing is correct. Manufacturing exports are only half as NO_x intensive as oil exports. For PT and SO_x, manufacturing is dirtier than oil production by a factor of 10 and 3 respectively. If Mexico had continued its earlier policies of relying on oil exports, and oil

TABLE **4.7** Air Pollution Intensity in Manufacturing vs. Oil Refining

	Oil	Manufacturing	Ratio (Manufacturing/Oil)
PT	0.06	0.58	10.02
SO_x	0.34	1.06	3.17
NO_x	1.59	0.72	0.45

SOURCE: Author's calculations based on (UNIDO 2000; World Bank 2000).

exports grew at the same rate as manufactures exports actually did grow over the same period, there would be much more PT and SO_x pollution, and less NO_x pollution.

The second counterfactual question is: What if Mexico had undertaken its 1985 and 1987 reforms, but not NAFTA? To examine this question the annual changes in scale, composition, and net effects are examined for the three pollutants discussed in this chapter. The results are presented in Table 4.8.

The first column pre-NAFTA, exhibits the annual scale, composition, and net effects for each pollutant (and the average of all three) from 1984 to 1994, from just before Apertura until NAFTA was signed.

TABLE **4.8** Pre-NAFTA vs. Post-NAFTA Changes in Pollution

	Pre-NAFTA	Post-NAFTA	Full Period
PT			
scale	−546	4,607	926
composition	−93	−470	−201
net	−639	4,137	725
SO_x			
scale	−994	8,390	1,687
composition	−1,188	−569	−1,011
net	−2,182	7,821	676
NO_x			
scale	−672	5,672	11,140
composition	−221	597	13
net	−893	6,270	1,153
Average			
scale	−738	6,223	1,251
composition	−501	−147	−400
net	−1,238	6,076	851

SOURCE: Author's calculations based on (UNIDO 2000; World Bank 2000).

The second column shows the annual trends pollution change in the post-NAFTA period. The third column has the full period, 1984 to 1998 for comparison purposes.

Comparing the first two columns answers the counterfactual. During the pre-NAFTA period both the scale and compositional effects of pollution were declining for all three pollutants. This is the result of two phenomena. First, manufacturing growth as a whole dropped by 10 percent over this period, causing a reduction in the scale effect. Mexico had a severe crisis in 1985 that lasted through 1987. Second, the composition effect is negative because the share of criteria air pollution intensive industries began to decline.

During the years following NAFTA, Mexico's economy began to grow again, leading the scale effect to dramatically increase. This is shown in column two. For all three pollutants (and their average) the annual change of pollution is quite large. On average, the composition of Mexican industry continued to become cleaner, but such this is completely swamped by the scale effect. Of the two pollutants that did see a reduction in pollution intensity (composition effect) in the post-NAFTA period, PT decreased faster in the post-NAFTA period but SO_x decreased at a slower rate.

Without NAFTA, both the scale and composition effects of criteria air pollution in Mexican industry were decreasing. After NAFTA, the scale effect increased significantly while the composition effect continued to decrease but at a slower rate (comparing the averages at the bottom) than in the previous period and nowhere near enough to outstrip scale related changes.

Summary

There is no clear improvement or worsening in levels of criteria air pollution in Mexican manufacturing during the period under examination. After correcting for a number of errors and inconsistencies, this chapter utilizes a dataset of Mexico-specific air intensities to analyze the scale and compositional effects of industrial development during Mexico's period of economic integration. Although there were found to be significant compositional shifts in Mexican industry away from pollution intensive sectors, the net effect of industrial development was an increase in industrial air pollution. Such conclusions should be taken with caution. Like its predecessors in the literature, this chapter has not analyzed the technique effect. With this caveat, corresponding to the calculations conducted in this chapter, the following tentative conclusions can be drawn from this analysis: the scale effect outweighed the composition effect; the pollution intensity of the Mexican economy as a whole decreased slightly, due to the composition effect; since the trade reforms began in the mid 1980s, Mexican industry has become relatively less pollution intensive. There has, however, been acceleration of total pollution because of the post-NAFTA scale effect.

5   Is Mexico a Pollution Halo? The Case of Industrial Air Pollution II

Most theories of trade and environment assume that developing country environmental practices are relatively worse than their developed country counterparts. Based on the available evidence, such an assumption seems plausible. Indeed, this chapter will show that, in terms of criteria air pollution, manufacturing in Mexico is significantly more pollution intensive than manufacturing in the United States. A handful of Mexican industries are, however, actually cleaner than their U.S. counterparts. Why is this so?

The previous chapter focused on the scale and composition of criteria air pollution intensive industry in Mexico, during Mexico's period of economic integration. This chapter creates a Harmonization Index (HI) that compares the air pollution intensity of Mexican and U.S. manufacturing to estimate a technique effect for Mexico. After creating the HI, an analysis is conducted that shows how differences in fuel use and energy technology explain relative levels of pollution intensity in the two countries.

The chapter is divided into three parts. The first presents the HI and identifies those industries that are cleaner or dirtier in Mexico than in the United States. The second part presents the results of regression analyses that attempt to determine the extent to which energy use and technology explain those differences. The third part presents conclusions and develops the framework that arises from the analysis. The appendix outlines the data and methodologies used for the analyses.

Creating a Harmonization Index (HI)

Measuring the ratio between Mexico and U.S. air pollution intensity offers a glimpse at the differences in technology and pollution in the two countries. The exercise reveals that there are some industries in Mexico that are less air pollution intensive than their counterparts in the United States. Unfortunately, such industries are on the decline, relative to other industries in the Mexican economy.

Standards for the pollutants studied are strikingly similar in both the Mexico and the United States. An interesting question to ask is: are emissions harmonized? To answer this question, the first task is to determine the extent to which levels of pollution intensity vary between the two countries. To such an end, an HI is created for sulfur (SO_x), nitrous oxides (NO_x), and particulate matter (PT) in each industry (Note: that these comparisons only incorporate emissions in factories, not off-site energy-related emissions).

The result is that industry in Mexico is 14 times more pollution intensive than is the United States; however, this is driven by the HI for the rubber and pulp and paper industries (which are 88 and 20 times more air pollution intensive than their U.S. counterparts). A second set of industries (automotives, beverages, and chemicals) are only two to four times dirtier in Mexico than in the United States. There are three industries where air pollution intensity is cleaner in Mexico than in the United States: iron and steel, aluminum, and cement. The HI in Figure 5.1 on a log_{10} scale. Industries that protrude above one are more air pollution intensive in Mexico; those where the bar turns downward are less air pollution intensive.

Table 5.1 shows that those industries that are cleaner in Mexico are declining as a share of total economic activity in Mexico. In 1984, 29 percent of industrial, value-added in Mexico resided in the cleaner industries, but in 1998 that share fell to 25 percent. The shares become more stark for exports and Foreign Direct Investment (FDI). The share of cleaner industries in total exports was 17 percent in 1984, but fell to 14 percent by 1998. In 1994, 33 percent of all FDI in Mexico went to

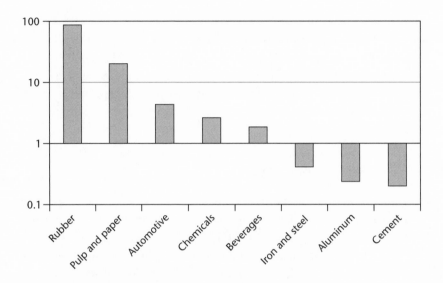

FIGURE **5.1** Harmonization Index (HI)

SOURCE: Author's calculations based on World Bank and UNIDO data.

TABLE **5.1** Share of Economic Activity in "Cleaner" and "Dirtier"
Mexican Industries (in percents)

	Cleaner		Dirtier	
	1984	1998	1984	1998
Production	29	25	71	75
Exports	17	14	83	86
FDI*	31	11	69	89

*1994.

industries that are cleaner than their U.S. counterparts; by 1998 that
share fell to 12 percent.

Cleaner *vs.* Dirtier Industries: The Importance of Plant
Vintage and Fuel Use

It is important to try and identify the factors that explain why
some industries in Mexico are cleaner than their U.S. counterparts. Identification of such factors could help reverse the trend shown in Table 5.1.

The subsequent analyses will show that pollution is, in large part, a function of plant vintage and fuel use. In industries where pollution is largely a function of core technologies and cleaner fuels, Mexico is cleaner than the United States. Those industries that use older technologies, burn dirtier fuels, and are more apt to need end-of-pipe technologies for pollution abatement are dirtier in Mexico when compared to the United States.

Estimating the Pollution Intensity of Industrial Manufacturing

This section outlines the major factors that have been shown to account for the pollution intensity of manufacturing in the world economy. The United Nations Institute for New Technologies has published a useful summary of technology and pollution intensity in manufacturing (Bartzokas and Yarime 1997). According to the study, which surveys production processes throughout the world economy, the environmental impacts of manufacturing have two sources: energy combustion emissions and byproducts of the production process itself.

Energy combustion is essential to various parts of the production process. As a result, air pollutants such as SO_x, NO_x, and PT are emitted at various levels, depending upon the amount of energy used and the type of fuel used for combustion. Some of the more energy-intensive industries are more capital intensive ones that transform matter from one form into another: iron ore and coke into steel, wood into paper products, bauxite into aluminum, and so forth. To reduce emissions from this part of the production process, newer combustion technologies are being developed that are more energy efficient and, thus, reduce the total amount of energy used. In addition, fuel-switching away from fuels like coal, diesel, and residual fuel oil and toward fuels such as natural gas lowers emissions. Table 5.2 exhibits emissions factors for such fuels in Mexico and the U.S. Table 5.3 shows the percentage of dirty fuels in Mexican and in U.S. manufacturing industries.

Although new technologies and changes in the fuel mix can reduce air pollution from energy in manufacturing, the main product and basic chemical reactions can remain unchanged. The chemical processes of paper bleaching, the paint mixing for automobiles, and wool dyeing are examples of production processes that create byproduct pollutants.

TABLE **5.2**   Air Pollution Emissions Factors for Fuel Use in Mexico

	Diesel	Residual Fuel Oil	Gas	Coal*
Sulfur	42.5	76	9.6×10^{-6}	28.50
NO$_x$	2.4	6.6	8.8×10^{-3}	5.80
PT	0.24	5.38	4.8×10^{-4}	n.a

*Emissions factors for US.

There are two strategies for byproduct pollution abatement. One strategy is use of end-of-pipe technologies (devices added to the final stage of production that remove waste). The second strategy is the use of process-integrated technologies that reduce or eliminate the creation of wastes themselves by making the production process more efficient through such activity as reuse and recycling, environmental management systems (EMS), or redesign of basic processes.

Cleaner Industries

Of the three industries in Mexico that are cleaner than their U.S. equivalents, plant vintage and cleaner fuel usage explain the difference for iron and steel, as well as for cement. In the case of aluminum, Mexico is cleaner because the Mexican aluminum sector is quite small and entails a much narrower (and less pollution-intensive) part of the production process compared to the United States.

Iron and Steel

The iron and steel sector is the clearest example of the relatively cleaner effects of plant vintage. During the years of economic integration, the Mexican steel industry was completely transformed. Beginning in the early 1990s, large new private investments, mostly domestic in origin, began to flow into the Mexican steel industry. Compared to the U.S. steel industry's notoriously slow growth (less than 1 percent annually), Mexican steel grew 3.7 percent annually in the 1990s. With such investment came newer, cleaner technologies. In addition, case study evidence has shown that some firms in the Mexican steel sector have begun to employ environmental management systems (Mercado Garcia 1999).

During the late 1980s, Mexico began to integrate its steel sector into the world economy by selling its state owned enterprises and by freeing the sector from government price controls. Adding momentum to this effort, in 1988 the World Bank gave the Mexican government a US$400 million loan to restructure the sector. Close to $170 million of the loan went to the modernization of technology and equipment at various steel facilities. In some cases, environmental clean-up and compliance were part of privatization agreements between government and private buyers (Gentry and Fernandez 1998).

A recent study on the diffusion of electric arc furnaces (EAFs) in the global economy included a variable as to whether each nation was considered open to foreign competition. Mexico, which has seen a surge in EAF production, was included in this study as an open nation—lending force to the article's conclusion that openness was correlated with the spread of cleaner energy technology in the world steel sector (Reppelin-Hill 1999). EAFs were a newer and more attractive technology choice for the steel industry when Mexico was privatizing (Mercardo Garcia 2000). In addition to being less capital intensive and therefore less costly, EAFs are significantly less air pollution intensive than basic oxygen furnaces (BOFs). In BOFs, coke, molten iron, scrap, and oxygen are used. Not all of these steps are used in EAFs, which primarily rely on scrap steel and electricity. It has been estimated that EAFs use one third of the energy used in conventional steel making (Nakajima 1993).

According to Mexico's National Association of Iron and Steel Industries, between 1990 and 1995 the average share of EAF in total Mexican production was 60 percent (CANACERO 2002). In addition, a number of dirtier blast furnaces were taken out of production. Indeed, 200 (relatively small) steel plants were taken out of production in Mexico between 1988 and 1998 (INEGI 2000). In the United States, EAFs were only 33 percent[1] of U.S. steel production (Crompton 2001). This observation makes it very clear that the vintage of Mexico's steel sector is an important factor explaining why Mexican steel is relatively less air pollution intensive than U.S. steel.

The fuel mix in Mexican steel is also much less air pollution intensive than in the United States. Only 10 percent of Mexican steel's fuel use

---

1. Averaging 1982 to 1987 to correspond with the IPPS data.

could be classified as "dirty" (see table 6.4), whereas almost 50 percent of the fuel in the U.S. steel industry is dirty (mostly coal). Many U.S. steel plants have been grandfathered into major air legislation in the United States because they are so old.[2] This comparison does not count electricity sector emissions, which makes the EAF look cleaner. Mexico's electricity sector is dirtier than in the United States. If these calculations included indirect emissions in electricity generation, this gap would narrow.

In addition to fuel use and plant vintage in Mexican steel, there are also signs that the industry is adopting a number of notable environmental policies. In a study of 12 Mexican steel plants, it was found that government regulation and foreign market pressure have triggered the industry to adopt EMS policies (Mercardo 2000; see also Gentry and Fernandez 1998).

Cement

The Mexican cement industry is another example of an industry that is more competitive than its U.S. counterpart. The Mexican cement industry has newer technologies, and has aggressive environmental management. Unbeknownst to some, Mexico's cement manufacturers own more cement plants than their counterparts in any other country. Mexican companies own 15 of the 51 major cement plants in the world.[3] The Mexican-owned plants produce 34 percent of world cement production. United States firms own 12 of the major cement plants and produce only 16 percent of global production capacity (CEMEX 2002). Between 1988 and 1994, years that coincide with the Mexico air pollution data, cement grew 4.6 percent annually in Mexico, compared to 3 percent growth in the U.S. (INEGI 2000).

Growth and competitiveness has allowed the Mexican cement industry to upgrade its technology. This is indicated in Table 5.3, which shows that the Mexican cement industry is almost twice as energy efficient as cement manufacturing in the United States. This is consistent

---

2. Grandfathering means that they are held to much less stringent standards than newer plants.

3. Not all Mexican-owned plants are in Mexico, some are in Spain, Egypt, Colombia, Thailand, and elsewhere.

TABLE **5.3**   Energy and Fuel Intensity

Sector	Mexico		United States	
	Energy (MJ/$)	Dirty Fuel (%)	Energy (MJ/$)	Dirty Fuel (%)
Iron and Steel	101.48	10	118.79	49
Chemicals	19.63	38	23.77	5
Cement	85.86	77	160.88	64
Pulp and Paper	37.45	39	40.36	21
Beer and Malt	6.41	41	5.36	38
Automotive	0.89	4	1.24	5
Rubber	7.38	27	4.47	8
Aluminum	31.36	0	169.98	1

SOURCE: Personal Communication, INEGI, 2002; Environmental Protection Agency, AP-42, 2002.

with other studies that have shown Mexican cement to be more energy efficient. According to the World Bank, between 1960 and 1980, Japan, Germany, and the United Kingdom's cement industries were more energy efficient than Mexico, but Mexican cement was one and one-third times more efficient than the United States (Fog and Nadkarni 1983). In a more recent study using plant-level data for 60 cement kilns in Mexico, it was found that the reduction in energy use per unit of output was due to new investment in capital equipment (Sterner 1990).

The Mexican cement industry has also taken a number of steps toward environmental management. Not all have been successful. During the 1990s, the Mexican cement industry worked with international consultants to certify its plants with internationally recognized environmental management systems (Lexington Group 1998). For these efforts and others like it, Mexico's largest cement company, CEMEX, was awarded the 2002 World Environment Center Gold Medal for International Corporate Environmental Achievement (CEMEX 2002). In some cases, such good intentions have displaced environmental problems rather than solve them. The Mexican cement industry has been involved in burning its hazardous waste as an alternative fuel in an attempt to save money and emit less criteria air pollutants, the pollutants under investigation in this chapter. As the emission of criteria air pollutants has decreased, the amount of toxic emissions has been shown to increase from the burning of hazardous wastes (TCPS 1997).

Aluminum

Mexico's aluminum industry is cleaner than aluminum production in the United States, for different reasons than in the steel and cement cases. As shown in Table 5.3, the aluminum sector is over five times more energy intensive in the United States than in Mexico. According to the HI, aluminum is cleaner than the United States for particulate matter (PT) and sulfur oxides (SO_x). Such a correlation can be deceiving.

In the Mexican aluminum sector it is not the case, like steel and cement, that growth has brought new investments and environmental management systems. In fact, from 1988 to 1994 the industry declined in Mexico, while the U.S. aluminum industry grew 6.3 percent annually (UNIDO 2002). Instead, the difference in pollution and energy intensity is a result of one thing: the United States is one of the biggest players in aluminum smelting in the world economy, while Mexico has a relatively small share of aluminum production, and specializes in rolling, casting, and secondary aluminum materials (UNIDO 2002; INEGI 2002).

Although smelting is absent in Mexico, in the United States it represents 34 percent of the total value of production. Smelting is vastly more energy and pollution intensive than the other parts of the aluminum production process. In the United States, smelting uses 86 percent of all energy in the aluminum sector. Also in the United States, smelting comprises 97 percent of all aluminum related SO_x emissions, and 98 percent of PT (DOE 1997).

Dirtier Industries

Among the eight industries under consideration, the industries that are significantly dirtier in Mexico are pulp and paper, rubber, chemicals, beverages, and automotive. On average, these industries are also more energy intensive in Mexico, and in some cases they are using much dirtier fuels and have relatively poor environmental records.

Referring back to the HI, the Mexican pulp and paper industry is very air pollution intensive when compared to its counterpart in the United States. On average, the Mexican pulp and paper sector is 20 times as dirty as the sector in the United States. A number of factors explain this: the type of fuels burned in Mexico, the pollution intensity of different parts of the production process in Mexico and the U.S., and the level of environmental regulation in the sector in each country.

Although Mexico and the United States have close to the same level of energy efficiency for pulp and paper, the Mexican industry uses relatively more dirty fuels than its U.S. equivalent. According to Table 5.3, 39 percent of the fuels used in Mexican pulp and paper are considered dirty, compared to 21 percent in the United States. In Mexico, most of the dirty fuels used are residual fuel oils, whereas little of dirty fuels in the United States are residual fuel oils.

The composition of the pulp and paper industry differs in Mexico and the United States, which also contributes to differing levels of air pollution intensity. In Mexico, almost 50 percent of all production in the sector is in pulp making and processing, and another 40 percent is the fabrication of packages and wrapping (INEGI 2000). Fifty percent of U.S. paper production is also in pulp making and processing, but only another 20 percent is in packages and wrapping (another 27 percent is in papermaking, UNIDO 2000). In Mexico, 40 percent of packaging and wrapping is in corrugated boxes, which is the most sulfur intensive part of the pulp and paper process. According to one study, production of corrugated boxes in the United States emits 28.3 pounds of sulfur per ton of product, while other parts of the production process only average 9 tons per ton of product (Tellus Institute 1992).

The Mexican pulp and paper industry may be subject to less environmental stringency than in the United States. Perhaps more than any other industry in this sample, pulp and paper making involves a myriad of production processes that create large amounts of byproduct waste (Tellus Institute 1992). Core technologies for pulp and paper-making have remained relatively widespread for half a century. Until the more sustainable production process found in places like Sweden diffuse throughout the world market, a large part of reductions in emissions must come from end-of-pipe technologies (Smith 1997). Indeed, under the U.S. Clean Air Act, the pulp and paper industry is required to install specific technologies to abate air pollution. Conversely, while pulp and paper falls under federal jurisdiction in Mexico, specific end-of-pipe technologies are not required (Baker and McKenzie 2000).

The other industries in the sample that are dirtier in Mexico (rubber, automotive, chemicals, and beverages) industries fit the general pattern of dirtier industries for Mexico: they are either more energy intensive or use dirtier fuels than in the United States. Although the rubber and automotive industries are significantly dirtier in Mexico than in the United States, they are the least air pollution intensive of those in the sample. Nevertheless, the energy intensity of Mexican rubber is 7.38 megajoules per dollar, while in the United States it is 4.47. In addition, 27 percent of the fuels used in the Mexican rubber industry are considered dirty, compared to only 8 percent in the U.S.

Given the limited amount of data available for both countries on this subject, it is somewhat difficult to confirm these findings statistically. Nevertheless, regression analyses were conducted (see Appendix) that partly confirm the discussions outlined above. These regressions show a clear relationship between energy use and pollution intensity (see Table A.1 in the Appendix).

Conclusions and Framework for More Research

There are a number of conclusions that can be drawn from this analysis that raise interesting questions for theory and policy:

- On average, Mexican industry is much more air pollution intensive than U.S. industry.
- The steel and cement sectors are cleaner than their U.S. counterparts.
- Those industries that are more air pollution intensive in Mexico are increasing as a share of total value added production, exports, and FDI.
- Supplementary analysis shows that in general, those industries that are less air pollution intensive in Mexico have succeeded in investing in newer, cleaner technologies, and burn less air pollution intensive fuels.
- Regression analyses imply that byproduct waste is strongly correlated with energy use in the United States, but in Mexico there is substantial byproduct intensity that is uncorrelated with energy intensity.

While this chapter has identified some patterns, more research in this area is desperately needed. This top down analysis that looks at aggregate levels of pollution and energy intensity would benefit greatly from the addition of a bottom up approach. While beyond the scope of this analysis, on the ground case studies of both the cleaner industries like steel and cement, in addition to the dirtier industries like pulp and paper would be the logical follow-up to this effort. In such case studies, it would be interesting to look at the different production technologies and processes, access the actual vintage of such technologies, and examine plant-level emissions.

This chapter raises interesting theoretical questions that are in need of more examination as well. This research suggests that when pollution is in large part a function of energy intensive technology, new investment from the integration process could bring environmental gain. On the other hand, when pollution is more a function of byproduct waste that requires end-of-pipe technologies, and such technologies are not required, new investment can be relatively worse for the environment. When the integration process causes firms to struggle, private funds do not exists for end-of-pipe and other environmental technologies. These observations lead to a larger hypothesis, summarized in Figure 5.2, that could be examined.

Here the Y axis is the capital-labor ration (K/L), and the X axis is the ratio of byproduct emissions to total emissions. The hypothesis could be defined as follows: in industries where pollution is a function of energy combustion technology, new investment will yield cleaner production; in

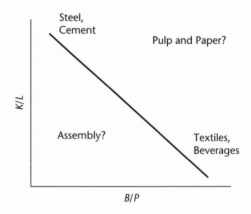

FIGURE **5.2**   The Economics of Pollution Intensity: A Hypothesis

industries where pollution is a function of end-of-pipe technologies, the effects of new investment are more ambiguous. The hypothesis is depicted in Figure 5.2. The pattern implicit in the hypothesis are those industries that fall along the trend line. The question is: If the data to adequately test the hypothesis were available, would sectors like pulp and paper, or even apparel, fit the pattern? Pulp and paper production is highly energy intensive and creates a significant amount of byproduct waste. Another question is: Would more sectors like apparel, which is not very energy or pollution intensive at all? These questions, in addition to sector specific research questions, present a vibrant research agenda that could follow from this study.

Harmonizing Up? The Development and
     Performance of Mexico's Environmental Policy

This chapter examines the evolution and effectiveness of Mexico's environmental policy in the context of economic integration. Mexico boasts a fairly wide array of environmental laws and institutions that date back at least to the 1980s. However, there has been a growing tension between economic and environmental policy in Mexico, where the latter has been forced to take a back seat in order to deal with the numerous economic crises that ensued during the same years.

This chapter is divided into four parts. 1) a short description of the origins and development of environmental policy in Mexico, 2) a review of previous studies on the effectiveness of Mexico's environmental policy, 3) a new analysis to the same end, and 4) a summary explanation for why Mexico's environmental regime has limited effectiveness.

The Development of Mexico's Environmental Policy

Mexico established its environmental regime at the same time that it began integrating itself with the world economy. Mexico has developed an environmental portfolio that includes a host of national laws, bilateral agreements with the United States, a trilateral agreement on environmental cooperation with Canada and the United States, and a number of Multilateral Environmental Agreements (MEAs). When Mexico began to cope with serious economic crises during its period of economic transformation, its development environmental policy began to slow, leaving it still in its infancy.

National Laws and Institutions

President de la Madrid (1982 to 1988) launched Mexico into serious environmental policymaking. After making the environment a campaign issue, the de la Madrid administration enacted the Federal Law of Environmental Protection in 1982. The Federal law contained chapters on air, water, and soil contamination; established penalties for violators of these laws; created a procedure for filing citizen complaints; and created air quality standards. In addition, the Ministry of Urban Development and Ecology (SEDUE) was established as Mexico's first cabinet level institution to have environmental protection as one of its purposes (OECD 1998). SEDUE is credited with undertaking a fairly extensive series of nationwide forums on environmental education that brought together local environmental officials, scholars, and Non-Governmental Organizations (NGOs) (Mumme, Bath et al. 1988; Mumme 1998). SEDUE also began conducting plant-level environmental inspections.

During the de la Madrid years, several hundred environmental NGOs began to mobilize. By 1985, these organizations organized into the first national environmental networks in Mexico (Dumas 1996). Such mobilization led to an increase in organized protest and lobbying activity that was coordinated in tandem with SEDUE's environmental forums. These efforts were often countered by the private sector, which urged the Mexican government to subordinate environmental protection to national development goals (Mumme, Bath et al. 1988).

Carlos Salinas took office in 1988. Like his predecessor, Salinas made the environment a presidential campaign issue (Mumme 1998). When in office, he immediately enacted what is referred to the General Law of Ecological Balance and Environmental Protection (LGEEPA) in 1988, which supersedes the 1982 law. LGEEPA became the legal foundation for all Mexican environmental protection. Some of the most significant regulations of this law were: Environmental Protection Regarding Environmental Impact; Environmental Protection Related to Hazardous Residues; Environmental Protection Related to the Prevention and

Control of Air Pollution; and Regulations for the Prevention and Control of Water Pollution. It also gave state and local governments the power to develop their own environmental regulations (Prati-Perugia 1993).

Perhaps the most important aspect of LGEEPA was Mexico's enactment, for the first time, of U.S. style environmental impact regulation. This law required approval for any new industrial activity performed in Mexico, whether public or private, that could potentially cause contamination. Among other sectors, in manufacturing, these regulations were said to explicitly pay attention to manufacturing, especially industrial chemicals, food and beverages, cement, and automotive industries.

In 1992, the Salinas administration absorbed SEDUE into a Ministry of Social Development in (SEDESOL). SEDESOL was buttressed by two complementary bodies, the National Institute of Ecology (INE), and the Federal Attorney for Environmental Protection (PROFEPA). INE sponsors environmental research in Mexico, PROFEPA is charged with enforcement. Finally, in 1994, the environmental arm of SEDESOL was split off to form the Ministry of Environment, Natural Resources, and Fisheries (SEMARNAP). INE and PROFEPA became housed there as well (OECD 1998).

It was also in the early 1990s, around the time of UNCED, that selected portions of Mexican industry began being pro-active on the environmental front. In preparation for UNCED, what was later to become the World Business Council for Sustainable Development (WBCSD) had been formed by many of the world's largest companies. The Latin American chapter of WBCSD was established shortly thereafter in 1993, with an office in the US border region. In 1992, the National Council of Ecological Industrialists (CONIECO) was created as an organization of manufacturers and resellers of products that can help clean the environment. Finally, in 1994, the Center for Private Sector Studies for Sustainable Development (CESPEDES) was formed (Barkin 1999).

Ernesto Zedillo's administration (1994 to 2000) left most of the environmental institutions untouched, but did preside over a key addition to the Mexican constitution that pertained to the environment. In 1998, a key paragraph was added to Article 4 that reads "all persons have the right to an environment appropriate for their development and well-being." However, as will be shown later in this chapter, when confronted with economic crises, Zedillo significantly reduced funding for environmental protection.

Although this study does not include an assessment of the environmental record of president Vicente Fox (2000 to 2006), a few developments should be noted. Fisheries issues have been moved to another ministry, thus SEMARNAP has been changed to the Ministry of Environment, Natural Resources and Land, SEMARNAT. Perhaps the most significant development was the passage, in 2001, of a Pollution Release and Transfer System (PRTR), which would require Mexican firms to report the use of toxic and criteria pollutants to the government and public. Although this program is mimicked after U.S. and Canadian PRTRs, Mexico's is seen as the strongest to date (Winfield 2003).

Bi-lateral Affairs with the United States

Mexico and the United States had been addressing their transboundary environmental disputes under the International Boundary Commission since 1889. The commission was replaced with the International Boundary and Water Commission in 1944 through a water treaty between the two nations (Gilbreath and Torra 1994). When the 1965 maquiladora program was instated however, the United States and Mexico entered into a period of border area industrial integration that resulted in a number of well documented environmental problems (OECD 1998).

In response to these problems, Mexico and the United States signed the La Paz Agreement on Cooperation for the Protection and Improvement of the Border Area (1983). The agreement established a framework for cooperation between the two countries to prevent, reduce, and eliminate sources of air, water, and land pollution along the zone extending 100 kilometers along each side of the border. Specifically, the agreement establishes a procedure for establishing annexes that facilitate cooperation on different environmental issues. There are five such annexes, on waste water treatment, emergency preparedness, transboundary movement of hazardous waste, copper and smelter emissions, and air pollution (Environmental Protection Agency (EPA)).

Also in bilateral affairs, the Integrated Border Plan (IBP) was signed between the United States and Mexico in 1992. A response to public outcry by Mexican and US NGOs and trade unions, the IBP targeted the environmental problems along the Mexico-US border (Mayer 98). Its goals were to strengthen enforcement of existing environmental law; reduce pollution through new initiatives; increase cooperative planning and education; and to increase informational exchange and data collection (EPA 2000). As part of the NAFTA package, a host of border institutions were agreed upon between Mexico and the United States as well. These institutions are the Border Environmental Cooperation Commission (BECC) and North American Development Bank (NADBANK). The two bodies were established to "develop, finance, and construct environmental infrastructure projects, with special priority for wastewater treatment, drinking water, and municipal solid waste projects." BECC is a technical assistance organization that aids communities in the short term to develop water supply, waste-water treatment, and solid waste management infrastructure, and to certify these projects for loans from NADBANK and others. NADBANK set up to disperse two to three billion dollars.

Trilateral Commitments

As discussed in Chapter 2, Mexico is one of three parties to NAFTA. The NAFTA agreement culminated in an environmental package that consisted of new national institutions for environmental protection, new bilateral environmental agreements and institutions with the United States (described above), environmental text in the NAFTA agreement itself, and a trilateral environmental agreement with the United States and Canada that also included a new trilateral environmental institution.

Mexico agreed to a number of environmental policies between Mexico, the U.S. and Canada. In response to pressure by the U.S. government, U.S. and Mexican NGOs, and the international media, the government of Mexico agreed to environmental provisions in the NAFTA text, and a trilateral agreement for environmental cooperation that establishes a three-nation environmental institution. These provisions were opposed by the private sector in the United States and Mexico ((EPA); Audley 1996; Alfie-Cohen 1998; Mumme 1998).

The three nations also signed a North American Agreement on Environmental Cooperation (NAAEC). NAAEC generally establishes a cooperation framework to, among other things, "enhance compliance with, and enforcement of, environmental laws, procedures, policies, and practices." NAAEC creates a tripartite institutional structure: the Commission for Environmental Cooperation (CEC), a Joint Public Advisory Council that consists of business, government, and environmental representatives (JPAC), and a Council of Ministers (the three nation's environmental ministries).

The NAAEC has three mechanisms intended to reduce the incentive for a Party to relax its environmental laws: Article 13–15 and Part V "Consultation and Dispute Resolution." Under Article 13, the Secretariat can prepare a report on any environmental issue related to trade among the Parties and submit it to the Council. The Council can then choose to make the report public. With Article 14, a submission from an NGO, firm, or individual can occur where the NGO asserts that a Party is failing to enforce environmental laws. After passing a set of criteria, the Council can order the CEC to conduct a factual record (Article 15) on the matter. With a two-thirds majority the Council can have a record made public upon completion.

Finally, in Part V of the NAAEC, articles 22–36, is where enforcement mechanisms fall. If any of the Parties of the Agreement sees another as regularly violating its environmental laws as a result of trade, a Party can go through consultation, arbitration, and reporting procedures in attempt to reverse the matter. If the many steps in this process continue to deem the Party under question as a consistent violator who will not remedy the problem, in the end, up to 20 million dollars worth of fines could be charged to the violating party. In the end, in cases where the accused Party does not pay their fines, then the violating Party can have its NAFTA benefits suspended (NACEC 2002).

Assessing Mexico's Environmental Policy: Review of Previous Studies

From the early 1980s to the end of the twentieth century, Mexico developed an impressive level of environmental laws and institutions. Were they effective? A handful of recent studies can shed light on this question but fall short of giving definitive answers. These earlier studies can be summarized as praising Mexico for developing an adequate environmental infrastructure that is capable of addressing environmental problems, but that is not necessarily equipped with the necessary resources and commitments to do so. Although some of the studies point to some significant quantifiable environmental gains, the majority of studies complain that Mexico is not giving their environmental regime the proper attention to meet the environmental challenges.

Reviews by the World Bank, the Organization for Cooperation and Development (OECD), the NACEC, think tanks, and academics have applauded Mexico for developing the environmental policies outlined in the last section. They point to a number of measurable improvements in Mexico's environmental quality and policy, such as: reductions in levels of lead and carbon monoxide (CO) in Mexico City's airshed, the creation of a system (with an accompanying endowment fund) for biodiversity preservation, improvements in the amount of safely handled hazardous wastes, and greater environmental awareness and compliance by large firms in Mexico's business community (Husted and Logsdon 1997; OECD 1998; Dasgupta, Hettige et al. 2000; Hufbauer 2000; World Bank 2001; NACEC 2002).

Despite these gains, the same assessments highlight the many signs of severe environmental degradation that continue to occur in Mexico. The World Bank reports that, among other problems: less than ten percent of wastewater from industry, agriculture, and households is properly treated; barely 35 percent of solid and hazardous waste is disposed of in a sanitary manner; and dramatic losses in biological and genetic diversity are occurring. In the case of air pollution, the Bank concludes, that despite the existence of dedicated institutions, Mexican "structures, mandates, and resources remain weak or insufficient" (World Bank 2001, 694). Separate reports have echoed the point about losses in biological and genetic diversity, especially in the context of corn production (Nadal 2001; Quist and Chapela 2001). It has also been shown that, although there has been some gain in the amount of safely treated hazardous waste, only 6.5 percent of the 3.6 million tons of hazardous waste is handled safely (Hufbauer 2000). In the U.S.-Mexico border area, economic activity and population growth have grown to exceed the capacities of public infrastructure, which has led to inadequate water and sewage supplies, and harsh effects on habitats and biodiversity (OECD 1998).

Effectiveness of Mexican Environmental Policy

Consistent with the earlier research, the analysis in this chapter shows that Mexico's environmental regime still falls short of being fully effective, which is worsening many adverse environmental problems. To assess the effectiveness of Mexico's environmental regime from 1985 to 1999, this section examines overall levels of environmental degradation, as well as levels of pollution intensity in the Mexican economy; examines overall levels of regulation and enforcement; the amount of spending on environmental protection; the use of environmental management systems by private firms; and the level of public scrutiny on environmental matters in Mexico.

Pollution Intensity

Even if total pollution is still growing, environmental policies can trigger reductions in the level of pollution intensity in an economy that could lead to lessened environmental degradation in the future. Pollution intensity is the amount of pollution (or environmental degradation) divided by the nation's Gross Domestic Product (GDP). If effective policy causes reductions in pollution per unit of output at a rate that is faster than economic growth one can expect an increase in total pollution, but at a decreasing rate. This section will show that this is not occurring in Mexico.

As we saw in Chapter 2, overall levels of key environmental problems continue to worsen. According to the Mexican government, between 1985 and 1999: rural soil erosion grew by 89 percent, municipal solid waste by 108 percent, water pollution by 29 percent, and urban air pollution by 97 percent. For the same environmental indicators, Figure 6.1 calculates pollution intensities for Mexico. For each environmental indicator, physical units of environmental degradation (tons for soil, solid waste and air pollution, millions of cubic meters for water pollution) are divided by the Mexican GDP (in $US1995).

Figure 6.1 shows that the intensity of water pollution has indeed declined during the period examined in this volume. Water intensity is down 10 percent since 1985 and the other three indicators rose by 35 to

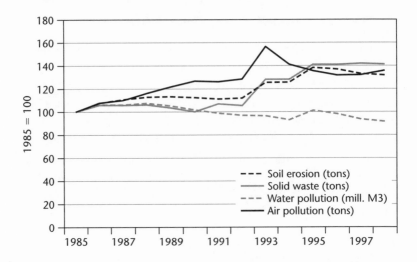

FIGURE **6.1**   Pollution Intensity of the Mexican Economy

40 percent. Even in the case of water, however, reductions in intensity are not as fast as economic growth. This shows that environmental policy is not only falling short of reversing the overall environmental trends in the Mexican economy, it is also falling short in reducing the rate at which degradation will occur in the future.

Spending on Environmental Protection

A key determinant of firm-level compliance with environmental regulations is the amount of funds dedicated to environmental protection. A related question for Mexico has been whether firms can mobilize or gain access to the necessary funds to modernize their energy and production equipment, install end-of-pipe technologies, switch to less environmentally damaging fuels, initiate cogeneration programs, and establish environmental management systems.

Figure 6.2 presents real (government) spending on environmental protection from 1985 to 1999. Spending grew impressively between 1988 and 1993, but then tapered off by 45 percent after NAFTA went into effect. Although spending on the environment has grown considerably compared to earlier levels, it remains the lowest of all OECD

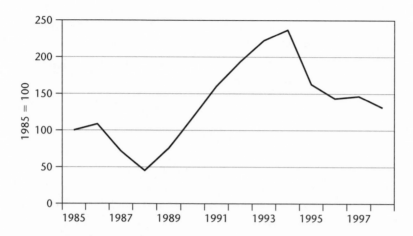

FIGURE **6.2**   Real Spending on Environmental Protection
SOURCE: INEGI 2000.

countries. In relation to GDP, the average OECD country spends three times more than Mexico on the environment (OECD 1999). Firms have been therefore left to their own devices to comply. For this reason, the record has been mixed.

World Bank and OECD studies have reported that large firms in Mexico are more likely to comply with environmental regulations than small firms (OECD 1998; Dasgupta, Hettige et al. 2000; Nadal 2001; Quist and Chapela 2001). Large firms are easier for governments and citizen groups to monitor, and should have lower costs for environmental compliance at the margin. Larger firms are also more apt to be the recipients of Foreign Direct Investment (FDI), which can bring newer environmental technologies. The World Bank study found large firms to be more often in compliance than smaller ones, but found no link between FDI and compliance. Other studies have found the Mexican steel and chemical fibres sectors to be in relative compliance with law, to a certain extent due to environmental management systems (like ISO 14000) and foreign direct investment.

Many firms could not voluntarily increase levels of compliance—many industries were growing very slowly or not growing at all and simply could not afford to step up environmental protection. An example is the Mexican textiles industry. Textiles production dropped during the period of trade opening, and funds were not available for environmental management. When funds were appropriated for environmental management in the textiles industry they were a result of government and community policing activities (Brown 2000).

Enforcement

It is common knowledge that firms that are subject to government enforcement and inspection measures are likely to be significantly cleaner than their counterparts. Based on surveys of 236 industrial firms in Mexico, the World Bank (mentioned above) found that regulatory requirements and enforcement were a primary reason why those firms were in compliance with environmental regulation in 60 percent of the firms surveyed (Dasgupta, Hettige et al. 2000).

Mexico's overall record on enforcement and inspections has been very poor. Figure 6.3 shows that after years of very scant amounts of plant-level environmental inspections, Mexico began to emphasize enforcement during the NAFTA negotiations, presumably due to pressure from its negotiating partners (or a desire to win over opponents of

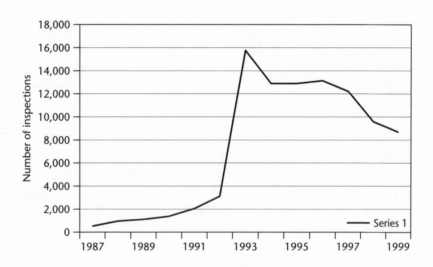

FIGURE **6.3**   **Plant-level Environmental Inspections**
SOURCE: PROFEPA 2000.

NAFTA). Although the trend was going in the right direction, reaching its highest point in 1993, plant-level environmental inspections peaked at only six percent of all firms in the country (PROFEPA 2000). What is worrisome is that after NAFTA was passed, the number of plant-level inspections began to diminish precipitously (falling 45 percent below the peak by 1999), suggesting that since NAFTA Mexico has become less serious about enforcement.

Although the overall trends in enforcement in Mexico are disappointing, there are a few success stories. There is evidence that a large number of inspections were concentrated in a few industries, mainly the chemical-petrochemicals, metallurgy, and pulp and paper industries. Positive results have been documented in the chemical fibres, and steel industries. In addition to government enforcement, such gains were also due to external influences and market pressure. In these two industries, changes in environmental management were also in part because their foreign owners, customers, or governments in foreign markets demanded such measures (Dominquez-Villalabos 2000).

In addition to these successes, the Mexican government has started a Clean Industry program that offers the carrot of voluntary compliance as opposed to the stick of inspections. To qualify for this program, a firm must permit an independent auditor to conduct an assessment of the plant's environmental performance (Gilbreath 2003). After the assessment is completed, the firm signs an agreement with PROFEPA and officially enters the program. When the firm meets the goals outlined in the agreement (starting with full compliance) they become certified and are not subject to inspections. Firms have to be re-certified every two years and after they reach compliance they are encouraged to go beyond compliance.

Community Pressure

Scrutiny by local communities has also been found to exert significant influence over the environmental behavior of Mexican industry. The World Bank study shows that public scrutiny has been an effective tool to steer industrial firms toward environmental compliance. Indeed, public scrutiny was found to be an important driver of environmental compliance in 25 percent of the firms showing improvements in the sample (Dasgupta et al. 2000). This effect was particularly strong for firms that were publicly traded. The logic is that firms that are traded publicly are held more accountable because news of environmental performance can more easily affect their stock performance (Dasgupta et al. 2000). Because of data limitations, it is difficult to gauge the level of community pressure on industry in Mexico. Some case study evidence has shown that community pressure has been a key driver of environmental compliance in Mexico, and may be growing (Wise 2003).

This section has outlined the state of Mexican efforts toward improving compliance toward environmental regulation. The overall trends are quite poor. Levels of enforcement are decreasing, and few additional funds are available for pollution control. There are signs of improvement in a few key polluting sectors, such as chemicals and steel. In these two cases, a blend of enforcement, private investment, and community pressure have been the drivers of increasing levels of environmental performance.

NACEC to the Rescue?

This chapter has shown that environmental conditions continued to worsen in Mexico during the post-NAFTA period, at considerable cost to Mexican society. Mexico chose not to steer the benefits of economic integration into increasing environmental protection. Such a finding leaves a clear role for the development of environmental institutions as part of trade and investment treaties. If a fully-equipped environmental institution was established to help Mexico meet its own environmental goals, Mexico may have been able to enjoy more of the benefits of economic integration.

NACEC, however, is ill-equipped to help solve Mexico's significant environmental problems. In addition to lacking the necessary mandate, NACEC lacks resources to counter these problems. By its very nature, an institution with an annual budget of $9 million can hardly make a dent in a series of problems that cost the Mexican economy over $40 billion annually. Although NACEC is not equipped to reverse overall trends, it has made a number of significant strides in some areas.

The actual amount of funds spent by NACEC on environmental projects is less than half of the $9 million; the projects budget is closer to about $3 million per year. Additionally, another $1 million supports the North American Fund on Environmental Cooperation (NAFEC), discussed later in the chapter. Remembering that the estimated environmental costs of air pollution in Mexico amount to over $25 billion annually (see Chapter 3), the author conducted an analysis of NACEC budgets to estimate the amount of funds earmarked for air projects. Since NACEC's inception, I estimate that $2 million in grants and loans (about $200,000 in loans) have gone to air related projects (NACEC 2000).

On the other hand, NACEC has set an important precedent for trade policy. Because of NAFTA's incorporation of environmental considerations, trade policy is no longer seen as separate from environmental policy (Marc-Johnson and Beaulieu 1997). Although NACEC was not designed to significantly reverse the environmental consequences of economic growth in Mexico, it serves as a pilot project to examine how effective institutions could be designed for Mexico and other nations where trade-led growth needs to be channeled in a more environmentally benign manner. A few of NACEC's programs for increased funding, monitoring, and citizen participation deserve note.

NACEC's Fund for Pollution Prevention Projects in Mexican Small and Medium Sized Enterprises (FIPREV), and its North American Fund for Environmental Cooperation (NAFEC) are both new sources of funds for industry and communities. Although these funds do not have adequate resources to significantly reduce the environmental costs of industrial growth in Mexico, they serve as models for Mexico and for mechanisms that could be established in the context of the FTAA.

Created in 1996, FIPREV is a pilot fund for pollution prevention projects in small and medium sized enterprises in Mexico. After an initial period of assessment, the fund now has over $2 million, and has given over 25 loans amounting to $610,000. Not only did NACEC provide funds for FIPREV itself, but was able to leverage funds from other sources.

FIPREV was established through a collaboration with the Mexican Fund for Technology Transfer in Small and Medium Sized Enterprises (FUNTEC). FUNTEC is a non-governmental organization linked to the Mexican Federation of Industrial Associations (CONCAMIN). FIPREV was founded to "promote the use of pollution prevention techniques and technologies among small and medium sized Mexican industrial establishments and support them in the development of their environmental management capacities," and to "facilitate the application of pollution prevention measures in industry through the timely and appropriate offering of technical assistance, information, and financing for projects of this nature." (NACEC 2001). The administration of FIPREV brings together members of business, academia, government, and representatives of NACEC's Joint Public Advisory Committee (JPAC).

Based on a series of preliminary needs assessments, the majority of FIPREV's projects are in the tanning industry, however other loans have been granted to firms in the food, metalworking, electroplating, chemicals, foundry, dry cleaning, and other manufactures. FIPREV's low interest loans can amount to $30,000 or 80 percent of an investment project. They are most often offered in Mexican pesos but can come in the form of U.S. dollars if the firm is exporting its goods or services. To date, most of these loans have come in the form of technical assistance to firms to make process-based technological changes to reduce water and raw materials usage. Impressively, of the 25 loans thus far granted by FIPREV, all firms have repaid both the credit and interest according to schedule. Based on the annual savings of approximately 1,465 tons of chemical substances, FIPREV estimates that the economic benefits of these environmental programs have amounted to $646,000 each year since their inception.

NAFEC was also established by NACEC in 1996, and its mission is to provide grants to community-based NGOs for social and environmental projects in the three countries. Since its inception, NAFEC has issued over 142 grants for a total of $5.4 million. The average grant is approximately $30,000.

Relatively few grants have been issued to help communities monitor Mexican industry. Little more than $200,000 has gone toward projects related to industrial pollution in Mexico. However, the grants that have been issued for community-based monitoring of industrial activity have been quite effective. In 1998, $50,000 was given to the U.S. based Environmental Health Coalition for a U.S./Mexico Comparable Industries Study on pollution prevention. Under this grant, a number of U.S. and Mexican NGOs worked together to identify the toxic chemical uses at three maquiladoras. Short fact sheets were put together based on the findings and distributed to the public to encourage their involvement in subsequent negotiations with the companies. Indeed, the groups then entered into negotiations with those firms to reduce emissions and to implement pollution prevention strategies.

In 2000, grants totaling $45,000 were issued to a Mexican NGO named Enlace, Ecologico in Agua Prieta, Mexico. The grant was given for the community use of the Pollutant Release and Transfer Registry in Mexico. Enlace Ecologico created a pilot project in Agua Prieta and Nogales to test how NGOs can monitor and list pollutant releases in their communities. The groups will then work with 100 maquiladoras to assist them in reporting their pollutant releases. Industry leaders and community members will then be encouraged to create ongoing monitoring systems and dialogue concerning abatement strategies.

NACEC has two mechanisms that provide additional means to monitor the enforcement of environmental laws in North America. Articles 14 and 15 of NAAEC allow citizens to make submissions to NACEC regarding the failure of a NAFTA party to enforce its environmental laws. Article 22 allows any of the three NAFTA governments to enter into a dispute resolution process with parties that persistently fail to enforce environmental laws.

Under Articles 14 and 15, if a submission is accepted by NACEC, NACEC commissions and publishes a factual record. If a factual record deems that environmental law was continually violated, there are no requirements that action has to be taken. It is hoped that increased public attention to the matter will trigger government action. There is evidence to suggest that such public attention can induce change. The NGO that issued the submission that resulted in the factual record to investigate alleged violations due to the development of the Cozumel Pier has gone on record to say that the factual record led to improvements in environmental impact assessment, and the eventual establishment of a fund for reef protection. For Article 22, nations found in violation can be fined and after a long process can eventually have NAFTA privileges suspended. Citizen submissions have been issued for cases related to industrial pollution in Mexico but thus far Article 22 has not been exercised at all.

According to Mexico's General Law of Ecological Equilibrium and Environmental Protection (LGEEPA), all firms must file an environmental impact statement upon establishing operations. Once a firm is in operation, there are a number of standards that are required, including a series of norms for air pollution. As one example, the submitters allege that Molymex failed to conduct an environmental impact assessment of its operations. In addition, the submitters claim that the plant is violating

Mexican standards that establish limits for SO_2 and particulate matter of ten microns or less (PM10).

A factual record will be conducted for this submission. Regardless of its outcome, it serves as a clear example of citizen-based efforts to supplement enforcement activities regarding industrial pollution in Mexico. Earlier in this chapter, we saw that Mexican efforts toward environmental inspections are on the decline. Articles 14 and 15 offer a way to counter that trend.

In addition to providing additional funds and an additional forum to monitor environmental enforcement efforts, NACEC also serves as a meeting place for cooperation, research, and information-sharing among the three countries. Before NAFTA, there were limited opportunities for trilateral activities of this nature (Mumme 1998).

Given its limited budget, perhaps NACEC's largest contribution is in the realm of enhancing environmental cooperation among the three governments. NACEC's five program areas (Environment, Economy, and Trade; Biodiversity and Ecosystems; Pollutants and Health; Capacity Building; and Law and Enforcement Cooperation) have all served as forums for governments and civil society to convene on their respective issues.

Highlights among these projects have been the development of a framework methodology for assessing the environmental impacts of NAFTA, which resulted in a number of commissioned studies that were presented at a NAFTA Effects Conference held by NACEC in 2000; the development of a North American Biodiversity Information Network; work toward the development of a North American Pollutant Release and Transfer Register as well as a North American Air Emissions Inventory; the development of a capacity building program for pollution prevention that links the work of FIPREV with similar activities in the United States and Canada; and a North American Regional Enforcement Forum that brings together experts to discuss efforts to create better incentives for environmental enforcement.

Summary and Conclusions

This chapter has shown that the development of environmental policy in Mexico failed to occur at a pace strong enough to address many of the environmental harms that came with trade-led growth. This is, in large part, due to the fact that Mexico's environmental regime was erected at the same time that Mexico was spending a great deal of effort to dismantle one economic system and replace it with a new one, and to cope with the economic crises that ensued alongside that transformation.

This chapter shows that:

- The pollution intensity of the Mexican economy is increasing significantly.
- Real spending on environmental policy has dropped by 45 percent since NAFTA, and Mexico spends the lowest on the environment of all OECD countries.
- The number of plant-level environmental inspections has decreased by 45 percent as well.
- NACEC is ill-equipped to fill environmental gaps in Mexico, but has a number of programs that could serve as pilots for more effective international trade and environmental institutions.

In many ways, it would be a lot to expect Mexico to develop a strong environmental regime at the same time that it was completely transforming from a closed to an open economy. Such a task was exceedingly difficult, as Chapter 2 shows, because the period of transformation has also coincided with severe macroeconomic crises, and increasing poverty and inequality. Mexico's environmental policy was crowded out by the economic problems that have occurred in Mexico during the same period.

7   **Bring the State Back In: Enabling National
Environmental Policy**

This study has tested the prevailing theories about the relationship
between economic integration and environment for Mexico. Mexico is
particularly well-suited for such an analysis because it began to integrate
into the world economy much earlier than many of its developing country counterparts, and because data for Mexico is relatively more prevalent than for other developing countries. On a national level, a number of
environmental conditions worsened in Mexico despite the rising incomes
that prevailing theories predicted would trigger reductions in environmental degradation. This has not occurred because dirty industry in the
United States flocked there. Environmental degradation worsened because the Mexican and U.S. governments did not instate adequate environmental policies that would have coupled environmental benefits with
economic integration.

The conclusions presented in this book suggest that there is a need
for a more scholarly evaluation of the role of the nation state during the
integration process and the extent to which environmental considerations should be incorporated into international trade and cooperation
agreements. Specifically, this study underscores the need for nation states
in the developing world and international institutions to address market
failures related to environmental externalities.

Judging from Mexico's experience, developing country governments need not fear that linking environmental protection to trade

liberalization will hurt their prospects for economic growth. The fact that Mexico did not serve as a pollution haven for heavily polluting firms from the United States suggests that the costs of compliance with environmental protection are not large enough to affect plant location decisions for the majority of firms. Therefore, it appears that if developing countries enact and enforce the appropriate environmental standards they will not scare away foreign investment during the process.

This final chapter is divided into three parts: 1) a restatement of the central research questions, a summary of the major findings, and a discussion of future research possibilities; 2) a discussion of the wider, theoretical implications of this; and 3) presentation of policy-related implications.

Summary of Results

The overarching research question for this book was: to what extent has economic integration coincided with environmental degradation in Mexico? This study examined the period between 1985 and 1999. Mexico began integrating itself with the world economy in 1985, and by 1999 it had become one of the more open economies in the world. More specifically, the author tested the two prevailing theories in the trade and environment literature, the Environmental Kuznets Curve (EKC) hypothesis and the "pollution haven hypothesis." In addition, the author conducted a case study of criteria air pollutants in Mexican manufacturing to examine the scale, composition, and technique effects of economic integration.

The context and background for this study is Mexico's transition from ISI to openness. By the 1970s Mexico became an enviable developing country, reaching growth rates that many developing countries still only dream of. By 1982, due to over-expansive macroeconomic policies, such progress came to a halt. As a strategy to get out of the 1982 crisis Mexico began to integrate itself into the world economy. Mexico is now a full-fledged General Agreement on Tariffs and Trade (GATT) member, a member of North American Free Trade Agreement (NAFTA), a member of the Organization for Economic Cooperation and Development (OECD), and a leading advocate for free trade at the World Trade Organization (WTO).

Economic integration brought mixed results to Mexico. Economic integration succeeded in stimulating both trade and investment, and it helped bring inflation under control. Indeed, between 1985 and 1999 Mexico's exports grew at a rapid annual rate of 10.6 percent in real terms, and foreign direct investment nearly tripled, posting a real 21 percent annual growth rate. On the other hand, many economists argue that such benefits did not accrue to the population as a whole. Mexico experienced less than one percent annual growth in Gross Domestic Product per capita from 1985–99, compared with 3.4 percent from 1960–80.

The remainder of this book examined some of the environmental consequences of these economic changes. Chapter 2 tested the EKC hypothesis for Mexico. According to the EKC, environmental degradation may sharply increase in the early stages of economic development, but a rise in per capita income past a certain turning point often said to be between $3,000 and $5,000, would gradually reduce environmental damage. Mexico reached $5,000 GDP per capita in 1985, precisely the year it began integrating into the world economy—thus it served as a perfect laboratory to test the EKC. The analysis in Chapter 2 found no sign of an inverted-U relationship between economic growth and environmental degradation in Mexico for the all the pollutants examined. This was true even for criteria air pollutants, which have been shown to have an EKC relationship in developed countries. If there is an EKC for Mexico, the turning point must be well above current income levels. It was found that carbon dioxide (CO_2) emissions, though increasing much faster than income, have done so at a decreasing rate. Based on these trends it could take between 10 and 60 years to reach a turning point for this pollutant.

Chapter 2 also showed that, based on official estimates from the Mexican government, the economic costs of environmental degradation in Mexico have been very significant. From 1985 to 1999 such costs have averaged 10 percent of annual GDP, or $36 billion per year. This trend stands in stark contrast to economic growth during that period, which only stood at 2.6 percent annually, or an increase of $9 billion per year. Air pollution is the most costly form of contamination in Mexico, representing 87 percent of the costs of environmental contamination. With these data on the economic costs of environmental degradation, and on trends in pollution from 1985 to 1999, the author estimated that Mexico's environmental degradation could continue to increase significantly into the future unless there is a dramatic change in Mexican environmental policy.

The author showed that if Mexico does end up experiencing an EKC, the turning point may not be for another 30 years, and could cost over $100 billion in today's terms.

However, these findings do not validate that increased environmental degradation in Mexico was due to Mexico serving as a pollution haven for U.S. firms. The author conducted numerous tests of the pollution haven hypothesis for Mexico, and all failed. High pollution abatement costs in the United States are not significantly correlated to the levels of economic activity in Mexico during the period of economic integration, 1984 to 1998 or to the changes in economic activity since NAFTA. The reason why such a result consistently appears in this study and others like it could be quite simple: even at the margin, the costs of pollution are too small to significantly factor into the average firm's location decisions. The marginal abatement costs are small related to the transaction costs of decommissioning and actually moving to another country. The results of Chapter 3 show that there was no widespread race to the bottom of dirty industries fleeing the United States to Mexico. These results have important implications for public policy.

Chapters 4 and 5 served as a case study of the scale, composition, and technique effects of criteria air pollution in Mexico's manufacturing sector. Chapter 4 looked at the scale and composition effects. Although there were found to be significant compositional shifts in Mexican industry away from pollution intensive sectors, the net effect of industrial development was an increase in industrial air pollution.

Chapter 5 estimated the technique effect for Mexico. In the absence of time series data for criteria air pollution in Mexican industry, the author created a Harmonization Index (HI) that compared the criteria air pollution intensity of specific manufacturing sectors in Mexico, with their counterparts in the United States. The purpose of this analysis was to examine the extent to which levels of technology and pollution were converging between the two countries. The author found that, on average, Mexican industry is much more air pollution intensive than U.S. industry. The steel and cement sectors are cleaner in Mexico than in the United States. Those industries that are less air pollution intensive in Mexico have succeeded in investing in newer, cleaner technologies, and burn less air pollution intensive fuels. Supplementary regression analyses provided further evidence of these findings by showing that byproduct waste is strongly correlated with energy use in the United States, but in Mexico there is substantial byproduct intensity that is uncorrelated with energy intensity. Unfortunately, these cleaner examples are more of an exception than a rule for Mexico. The author found that those industries that are more air pollution intensive in Mexico than in the United States, and are increasing as a share of Mexico's total value added, exports, and Foreign Direct Investment (FDI).

Chapter 6 showed that the development of environmental policy in Mexico failed to occur at a pace strong enough to address many of the environmental harms that came with trade-led growth. This is in large part due to the fact that Mexico's environmental regime was erected at the same time that Mexico was spending a great deal of effort to dismantle one economic system and replace it with a new one, and to cope with the economic crises that ensued alongside that transformation. Specifically, Chapter 6 showed that the pollution intensity of the Mexican economy is increasing significantly. Two key characteristics give an indication as to why this is occurring. Real spending on environmental policy has dropped by 45 percent since NAFTA. Second, the number of plant-level environmental inspections has decreased by 45 percent as well. North American Commission for Environmental Cooperation (NACEC), the institution erected as a result of the environmental side agreement to NAFTA, was ill-equipped to fill the environmental gap in Mexico. Chapter 6 did highlight a number of programs that could serve as pilots for more effective international trade and environmental institutions.

The findings in this book suggest a number of interesting avenues for further research. The most important follow-up would be to complement this fairly top down analysis that looks at aggregate levels of output and degradation with a bottom up approach that examines individual firms and sectors. Chapter 3 showed that the majority of pollution intensive industries are not moving to Mexico because of environmental concerns. There is some anecdotal evidence that some firms do cite environmental regulations as a key reason for their location decisions. Chapter 3 could be complemented by case studies of firms that did indeed move to Mexico because of environmental reasons. Such an analysis of firm-level decision-making at this level would shed light on the dynamics that trigger firm location decisions, and help policy-makers design policies that could deter firms for relocating for environmental reasons.

Similar case studies would also greatly enhance the analysis conducted in Chapter 5. On the ground case studies of both the cleaner industries like steel and cement, in addition to the dirtier industries like pulp and paper, would be the logical follow-up to that effort. In such case studies, it would be interesting to look at the actual production technologies and processes, determine the actual vintage of such technologies, and examine plant-level emissions. At the end of Chapter 5, the author discussed a possible hypothesis regarding the relationship between investment and the environment. The author hypothesizes that in those sectors where pollution is a function of plant vintage, new investment will lead to relatively less pollution. However, when pollution is more a function of end-of-pipe technology, new investment may not reduce pollution at all—especially if such technologies are not part of environmental policy in such a country. The data did not exist to test this hypothesis further, but such an analysis would be very interesting, even if conducted with data from the United States.

Implications for Theory

This study underscores the need to develop more comprehensive theories regarding the role of the developing country nation-state in the economic integration process. For close to 20 years, the prevailing emphasis of development theory has been the need to reduce government involvement in economic policy. In recent years, however, a number of scholars have begun to show how the nation-state can play a pro-active role in economic development. This study provides more evidence that the latter view is necessary, and provides insights as to the nature of state involvement that is needed for environmental policy.

As discussed early in Chapter 1, prevailing theories of trade and development emphasize the need to lessen the nation-state's role in trade and economic policy. The rationale for such an approach is that domestic and international markets, when left to their own devices, will work more effectively to promote trade and development than government policy will. Indeed, reducing the role of the nation-state became a key tenet of what become known as the Washington Consensus. The Washington Consensus, which also emphasized the need to liberalize trade and investment flows, was the prevailing recipe in the 1980s and

1990s that the U.S. government and the International Financial Institutions argued would bring development to developing countries.

Almost every economist agrees that markets can be efficient tools for allocating scarce resources for various ends, but most economists also agree that there are many areas where markets break down and fail—especially in developing countries. Now that a growing body of evidence is beginning to show the mixed results of the Washington Consensus, a burgeoning number of economists are arguing that there is a need to bring the state back in to development theory and policy.

Two economists have won the Nobel Committee Prize in Economics in part for showing that developing countries need the proper institutions in place in order to lay a good foundation for the development process. The first of these economists to win the prize was Douglas North, who showed that economic growth results from the development of institutions that buttress growth through the establishment of property rights and the establishment of contracts (North 1987). The need for property rights is a core tenet of environmental economics. Joseph Stiglitz, a more recent prize-winner, articulated that imperfect information flows are a key source of market failure and that developing countries especially need the institutions to correct those failures in order to develop (Stiglitz 1989). Recent empirical examinations confirm these theories. The economist Dani Rodrik and his colleagues have shown that the quality of institutions are the single most important variable in explaining the income growth of developing nations (whereas geography and trade have a relatively weak correlation with growth) (Rodrik et al. 2003).

A group of scholars outlining a theoretical justification for strong state involvement in economic transition stress the need for the government to exploit *positive* externalities with targeted economic policy. Authors such as Peter Evans (1995) and Alice Amsden (2001) have shown how many of the developing nations that experienced high growth and modest social development did so with strong government involvement (Evans 1995). These authors show how nations such as Taiwan, South Korea and to a lesser extent Brazil and India used a blend of state ownership, import duties, and subsidization to create handfuls of strong industries consciously linked to other parts of their economies. The rationale for such action was recognition of market failure: imperfect competition in the global marketplace was making it difficult for these nations to develop through a market-based strategy. By focusing government attention on industries such as high-technology electronics, these states created positive externalities that spilled over into other segments of their economies.

Relatively less attention is being paid to the need to address negative externalities such as environmental degradation during the reform process. The bulk of the academic work that does focus on negative environmental externalities emphasizes the need to reform and eliminate government policies that cause environmental degradation. Examples of this work include examinations of the extent to which subsidies in the energy, agricultural, and extractive resource sectors harm the environment. Many of these authors argue that the elimination of such subsidies and the privatization of state enterprises can create "win-win" scenarios that eliminate environmental harms and promote economic growth by making markets more efficient in developing countries (Blackman 2001).

In contrast to the growing number of scholars examining the need for a pro-active state to promote positive externalities, very few economists argue for a pro-active state in environmental policy-making in developing countries. The scant attention that is paid to these matters usually concerns the role that actors such as private firms and advocacy groups can play in protecting the environment in developing countries. Indeed, a recent survey of environmental issues in development economics has said, "given constraints on all kinds of conventional state-led environmental regulation in developing countries, the environment and development literature has increasingly focused on the potential for private-sector agents (such as community organizations, environmental advocacy groups, trade unions, stock markets, and consumers) to assume a leading role in pollution control" (Blackman et al. 2001, 5).

An exception to this rule is the work of Theodore Panayatou. Panayatou has argued for strong environmental policies on economic grounds (Panayotou 1993; Panayotou 1998; Panayotou 2000). For him, developing country governments should put proper environmental policies in place before environmental conditions begin to worsen, because prevention is far more cost-effective than abatement. In 1993, he wrote that the costs of pollution abatement and the stakes of the vested interests are higher after environmental degradation begins to occur. The new (post-degradation) economically-optimal level of pollution would leave a nation with more pollution than if it had a fresh start—after environmental degradation occurs it is most often technologically and economically not an option to achieve 100 percent abatement. Because of this economic and physical irreversibility, Panayatou has argued that the prompt internalization of external costs of production is both economically and environmentally preferable.

There is an emerging consensus among scholars that the gains from economic integration will be limited if a nation has not first put effective environmental policies in place (Esty 2001). Panayatou (1993) has shown how market failures in the environmental realm can distort developing country economies. He has shown that at least two fundamental conditions are required to make markets work well in a developing country. Property rights need to be defined that are exclusive, well defined, and enforceable. Prices in the marketplace should be set to reflect the true social costs of production.

Panayatou also shows how air pollution is a classic example of how poorly defined property rights and the presence of externalities can work together. Air pollution is an example of the misuse of an un-priced public good—clean air. The misuse of air due to the fact that it is a public good imposes a negative externality, pollution, on third party sectors and individuals. Moreover, the abatement of air pollution is also a public good. If one or even a handful of firms or individuals paid to abate air pollution, many more free riders would benefit from such abatement without having to pay. Panayatou argues that is the role of the state to act in the public interest to set fair and equitable burdens of pollution abatement on the public. Echoing the arguments of Douglas North, it is the role of government to establish the effective policies to define property rights and abate pollution.

Panayatou used this rationale in more recent writings in the wake of the EKC. In an article on the Environmental Kuznets Curve, Panayatou points out that many developing countries have yet to embark on establishing proper environmental policies, but stresses that it is important that they begin doing so, and sometimes on strictly economic grounds:

> "Since it may take decades for a low-income country to cross from the upward to the downward sloping part of the curve, the accumulated damages in the meanwhile may far exceed the present value of high

future growth. Therefore active environmental policy to mitigate emissions and resource depletion in the early stages of development may be justified on purely economic grounds." (Panayatou, 2000)

This study stresses and provides additional support for Panayatou's case. The author has shown how environmental degradation has come at great cost to the Mexican economy. Official Mexican government figures estimate that the economic costs of environmental degradation overwhelm the value of economic growth, which has been just 2.6 percent annually over the years studied here. Based on these costs, and on present environmental conditions, in Chapter 3 the author estimated that at current rates of growth it would take Mexico 30 years to reach a turning point for criteria air pollutants of $7,500 of income, and 99 years to reach the turning point of $15,000. The costs of the damage that would occur until Mexico reached the turning point could be as high as $279 billion, more than half of Mexico's total output in 2001. As Chapter 7 showed, the Mexican government has fallen short of putting the proper policies in place, even though a World Bank study showed how government inspections where among the key drivers of environmental compliance in the Mexican industry (Dasgupta, Hettige et al. 2000). There is a clear role for government policy to protect the environment in Mexico.

The results of my study lend support to Panayatou's arguments: more targeted spending on environmental protection for actions such as inspections will go a long way for developing countries. There are two additional economic rationales for charting such a path. Anderson (1992) has shown how developing countries can still gain from trade, even when they combine trade reform with optimal environmental policies.[1] Chapter 3's examination of the pollution haven hypothesis suggests that pollution-intensive firms will not be deterred from environmental policies. Installing environmental policy will not scare away foreign investment into countries like Mexico.

This section has made the theoretical case for a state role in environmental policy. However, what exactly then will enable states to do so from a policy perspective?

1. Runge notes that without the environmental properties that the gains from trade for a pollution-intensive industry can be greater (Runge, C. F. 1995). Trade, Pollution, and Environmental Protection. *The Handbook of Environmental Economics*. D. W. Bromley. Cambridge, MA, Blackwell.

Implications for Policy

This study lends support for the emerging consensus in economics that economic integration should be coupled with environmental policy in order to obtain the desired benefits of economic integration. Consider the following quotations from the World Bank and the WTO respectively. According to the World Bank, "increased trade and growth without appropriate environmental policies in place may have unwanted effects on the environment" (Frederikkson 1999). According to the WTO, "Trade would unambiguously raise welfare if proper environmental policies were in place" (Nordstrom 1999).

In a similar vein, I recommend four principles for trade and environmental policy based on the results of this study:

1. **Without the proper environmental policies in place, economic integration can exacerbate environmental problems.** This book underscores the need to have strong environmental policies in place before integrating. Developing nations fall short of establishing social and environmental policies in the face of economic integration for two reasons: because they are often in economic (and thus fiscal) crises that make few funds for social policy available; and that developing nations fear new social policies (especially environmental ones) may scare away foreign investment and domestic industry. Kym Anderson (1992) has shown that if environmental externalities are optimally internalized developing nations need not grow at the expense of the environment.

   This study has shown that dismantling government policies for environmental protection during the reform process has jeopardized the very goals of the economic reforms themselves. The integration process did not enable Mexico to couple economic and environmental policy, nor did Mexico seize the reforms as an opportunity. Esty (1997) has argued that the reform process is a unique opportunity to align economic and environmental policy during reform. Esty emphasizes that establishing the rule of environmental law; encouraging debate and the exchange of ideas through policies of transparency, accountability, and democracy; establishing domestic financing systems through market-based environmental policies; and exploiting positive environmental externality spillovers from FDI are all important first steps that should be taken (Esty 1997).

This book adds support and expands on this earlier work. Chapter 6 showed that the establishment of laws was not enough for Mexico. Mexico has passed numerous environmental laws, but the lack of enforcement of those laws has partially led to increases in environmental degradation. Therefore, the rule of law needs to be coupled with strong enforcement mechanisms.

The findings in this book suggest that it might have been economically prudent for Mexico to have invested a portion of its scarce and shrinking public funds toward environmental protection. Based on the principle that polluters should pay the cost of using scarce resources or causing damage to the productivity of resources, governments can use environmental taxation, trade-able permit systems, and other charge systems to raise funds while also giving them the incentive to pollute less (Panayatou 1998).

2. **Reserve the right to combine economic integration with strong environmental policy.** Developing countries should be given the room to move that can enable them to develop policies for social and environmental protection. This study suggests that if Mexico had combined economic reform with environmental policy it could have avoided enormous future costs and prevented harmful environmental degradation—without scaring away foreign investment and while still allowing for gains from trade. Developing countries need a diversity of tools to put the proper environmental policies in place.

The rules of economic integration should not be written in a way that will reduce the number of options available to developing countries who wish to reach these ends. Rodrik (2001) has shown that integrating an economy, especially into elaborate systems like the WTO and the NAFTA, can crowd out other institutional prerequisites for development such as maintaining property rights, exchange rates, and public health regimes (Rodrik 2001). Rodrik cites a World Bank study that has shown that it may cost the typical developing country close to $150 million just to comply with a handful of WTO disciplines (customs valuation, sanitary and phytosanitary measures, and intellectual property rights). That number is five times what Mexico spends on environmental policy annually.

3. **Well-designed environmental policies will not provide disincentives for foreign investment.** Using such instruments as those just described, if done properly, will not detract needed foreign investment from entering a developing country such as Mexico. The fact that this study, like so many others, finds no support for the pollution-haven hypothesis is good news for developed and developing countries alike. The marginal costs of pollution abatement are not significant enough to trigger firms to relocate (or change expansion plans) from one geographical region to another. Developed and developing countries are free to pursue environmental policies of the magnitude now in effect in developed countries without putting up barriers to economic growth.

4. **Substantial international cooperation should supplement developing countries' environmental goals.** This study has shown that Mexico did not have (or chose not to appropriate) the necessary funds to curb environmental degradation. Moreover, the international institutions created to help Mexico meet its environmental goals were not sufficient enough to fill the environmental gap created in the years examined for this study. During the NAFTA debates, the international community "demanded" that Mexico do more to protect its environment, but only ended up allocating a paltry $3 million per annum to that end. While developing countries can not and should not rely on the international community to finance its environmental priorities, it has been shown that the international actors can at least act as a catalyst that can help developing countries get their environmental priorities off to a good start while providing technical assistance and building the capacity of developing nations to eventually meet their own

goals (Esty 1997). Chapter 6 described how the Fund for Pollution Prevention Projects in Mexican Small and Medium sized Enterprises (FIPREV), North American Fund for Environmental Cooperation (NAFEC), and Pollution Release and Transfer Registry (PRTR) projects at NACEC also serve as good models for a more serious international effort toward effective trade and environmental policy.

It remains to be seen whether multi-lateral efforts will translate into significant improvements for Mexico. A major discussion in the trade and environment debates that was not largely discussed in this volume is the debate regarding the establishment of a world environmental organization (WEO) to counter the WTO. It has been argued that a WEO could synthesize existing multi-lateral environmental agreements and conceive of a series of uniform rules running across those agreements. If done in the proper manner, it is argued that a WEO would make it easier for developing countries to comply with MEAs and make it easier to develop environmental policies that are not in conflict with international trade rules. At this writing however, very little movement is occurring on the WEO issue (Esty 1994; Whalley 2001).

In both theory and practice, the goal of economic integration should be to maximize the possibility for development at the national level. This study on Mexico suggests that solely focusing on increasing levels of trade and international investment falls short of meeting such larger development goals—especially as they pertain to the environment. Such examination of Mexico will be useful as nations across the Western Hemisphere negotiate the proposed Free Trade Area of the Americas, and for the larger debates regarding the new round of global trade negotiations.

This book suggests that regional and global trading systems should be crafted as regimes to steer nations toward sustainable development, rather than away from sustainable development.

Technical Appendix

This section of the volume provides an explanation of the various calculations that were conducted in each chapter.

Chapter 2

Estimating Environmental Kuznets Curves (EKC) for Mexico

The calculations that estimate an Environmental Kuznets Curve (EKC) for Mexico involve simple least square regressions where the level of income and its square are regressed on environmental degradation per capita. To control for problems with serial auto-correlation, the first differences of the variables were also taken.

Estimating the Costs of Future Environmental Degradation

Parts of Chapter 2 estimate the amount and cost of environmental damage that would occur if Mexican environmental degradation began to turn around at possible EKC turning points of $7,500, $10,000 and $15,000 Gross Domestic Product (GDP) per capita. The amount of time and money it would take to reach each turning point is determined, in addition to the amount of time and money it would take to return to 1998 levels of pollution in Mexico, assuming the EKC is a parabola. Such calculations are performed in three stages. First, the number of years until Mexico reaches the respective turning points and returns to 1998 pollution levels is estimated. Second, the amount of environmental damage that would occur until the respective turning points and 1998 levels are reached is determined. Additionally, the present value of the environmental damage that would occur in the second stage is estimated. These calculations are expressed as follows:

if:

$$GDPCAP_t = GDPCAP_{98}(1 + g)^t$$

then:

$$\frac{GDPCAP_t}{GDPCAP_{98}} = (1 + g)^t$$

thus:

$$t = \frac{\log\left(\dfrac{GDPCAP_t}{GDPCAP_{98}}\right)}{\log(1 + g)}$$

hence:

$$TP = \frac{\log\dfrac{GDPCAP_t}{GDPCAP_{98}}}{\log(1 + g)}$$

Where (t) is time in years (1998 = 0), (TP) is the years to reach the turning point, (GDPCAP-TP) is the hypothesized turning point ($7,500, $10,000, and $15,000 in $1985 Purchasing Power Parity (PPP) to be consistent with the literature), and (g) is the GDP per capita growth rate. Although GDP per capita grew at an annual rate of .6 percent over the period, 1985 to 1999, the growth rate for the future has been increased to one percent.

The assumption of a parabolic EKC implies that the growth rate of pollution is linearly declining from its initial value to zero at the turning point (and negative values beyond the turning point). Thus, the author assumes that the pollution growth rate decreases annually by an amount equal to the average annual pollution growth rate from 1985 to 1999 (2.9 percent) divided by the number of years until the turning point is reached. The growth rate of pollution (P) in year (t) is expressed as ($\dot{P}_t$).

a) $\Delta \dot{P} = \left(\dfrac{\dot{P}_{(85-99)}}{TP}\right)$

b) $\dot{P}_t = \dot{P}_{t-1} - \Delta\dot{P}$

c) $P_t = (1 + \dot{P}_t)P_{t-1}$

Each year, the economic costs of environmental degradation is equal to the amount of pollution generated in that year multiplied by INEGI's estimate of the economic cost per ton of pollution which is $980 (this figure is consistent with similar World Bank studies on pollution abatement, see Hettige et al. 1994). These figures must be summed and discounted to estimate what Mexico would face as potential damages in today's terms. Such calculations are done to determine how much it would cost Mexico if it waited to reach potential turning points, and how much it would cost Mexico if it waited to get back to 1998 levels. The discount rates used were those recommended by the Intergovernmental Panel on Climate Change (IPCC) to estimate long term economic damages from global climate change, and are 3 and 6 percent (IPCC 2001).

Chapter 3

Chapter three empirically tests the pollution haven hypothesis. More specifically, the analysis in chapter 3 improves on previous work by examining whether the level of marginal pollution abatement costs in the United States has affected economic activity during Mexico's entire period of economic integration, pre- and post-North American Free Trade Agreement (NAFTA). This part of the appendix provides the model that is estimated for chapter 3, discusses the data and variables that are used, and ends with thoughts about the results that one would expect if Mexico became a pollution haven.

Most econometric examinations of the pollution haven hypothesis relate the level of economic activity in a range of manufacturing industries to conventional economic variables and to levels of marginal environmental abatement costs in those same industries in the United States or other countries with advanced levels of environmental regulation. This can be expressed as:

$$Y_{it} = \beta_1 + \sum_j \beta_{2j} X_{jt} + \beta_3 P_{it}$$

In this generalized model, the dependent variable (Y) is the measure of economic activity, often expressed as levels of value added production or exports (or their natural logarithms). The industrial branches that are examined are (i), and (t) is the time period that is considered. The dependent variable is regressed on a number of conventional economic variables (X_j), such as exchange rates, wages, interest rates and so forth, and a pollution variable (P). Betas are coefficients to be estimated.

This model examines whether an economy is becoming more pollution intensive by examining the effect of pollution (P) on levels of economic activity (Y), while holding the other factors that influence economic activity (X) constant. When examining this model for a developing country, evidence for a pollution haven would exist if the coefficient for pollution were to be found positive and statistically significant. In other words, on average, holding other factors that trigger economic activity constant, is the economy expanding relatively more in pollution intensive sectors?

For the analysis in this chapter, the basic model is modified to test the pollution haven hypothesis for Mexico. Because each industry in Mexico faces the same interest rates, exchange rates, and the other conventional macro-level economic variables (aside from wage rates) that affect production and trade (X), the analysis becomes a number of very simple bi-variate regressions of the above measures of economic activity on the pollution variables. These regressions form the crux of this chapter, and isolate the effect of levels of economic activity in Mexico during the period of economic integration on marginal pollution abatement costs. Among a cross-section of 27 manufacturing industries, 12 separate regressions are conducted with a single independent variable in each. There are six dependent variables measuring economic activity, and two independent variables that measure pollution abatement and levels of pollution. The model is expressed as:

$$\dot{Y}_{it} = \beta_1 + \beta_2 P_{it}$$

Here, ($\dot{Y}$) is a measure of the growth rate of economic activity, of which there are three measures used in this study: value added in Mexico, the value of exports in Mexico, and U.S. apparent consumption (see Table 4.3). Production data comes from the United Nations Industrial Development (UNIDO) 2000 Industrial Statistics Database (UNIDO 2000). Exports and apparent consumption data are from UNIDO's 2000 Demand-Supply Database. In each case, industries (i) are classified by three-digit Industrial Standard Identification Codes (ISIC).

These three measures of economic activity are split into two different time periods (t) for each industry (i). First, annual (real) growth rates from 1984 to 1998 were calculated for each of these three forms of economic activity. These three dependent variables allow me to examine whether Mexico became a pollution haven over its full span of economic integration. The second version is the increase (or decrease) in the annual growth rate after NAFTA. To create a set of dependent variables that could isolate the post-NAFTA period from the years previous to NAFTA, real annual growth rates in each industry from 1984 to 1994 were subtracted from real annual growth rates from 1994 to 1998. Thus, there are six dependent variables in all.

Each of these six dependent variables is regressed on a single independent variable of pollution. However, two different measures of pollution are used, so there are 12 regressions performed in total. The two separate pollution variables (P) are the marginal costs of environmental abatement in the United States, and an index that divides the air pollution emissions intensity for each industry in Mexico by the same measure for each industry in the United States.

To calculate the first pollution variable, marginal costs of environmental abatement in the United States, two World Bank databases were used. The Bank's Industrial Pollution Projection System (IPPS) provides pollution per unit of value-added output data for these industries in pounds per million 1987 dollars (Hettige, Martin et al. 1994). For many of the same pollutants in the IPPS dataset, the World Bank has provided a Costs of Pollution Abatement dataset as well (Hartman, Wheeler et al. 1994). For three-digit industries, the cost estimates are expressed in 1994 dollars per ton of pollution abated.

After making the necessary conversions from pounds to tons, and expressing each variable in 1994 dollars, calculating a variable for the marginal costs of pollution abatement in dollars of abatement costs per dollar of value added is a simple multiplication of the pollution coefficients (which are expressed in tons per dollar), by the cost coefficients (which are expressed in dollars per ton). The sum of all the marginal pollution abatement costs in the United States is less than one percent of value added production.

The costs for any individual pollutant are quite small, and the sum across all of these pollutants is consistent with other studies on the costs of pollution in the United States. Such studies find the average to be close to one percent, and the most costly to be 4.85 percent of value added. (see Levinson 1999). I found an average of .6 percent, with the most costly industry at 5.3 percent. Based on my calculations, five industries top the list as the costliest for abating pollution: pulp and paper (5.3 percent), chemicals (3.3 percent), non-ferrous metals (1.6 percent), tobacco manufacturing (1.4), and iron and steel (.8 percent).

The second pollution variable, based on pollution intensity rather than costs, was also created to test the pollution haven hypothesis for Mexico in separate regressions. The World Bank has also published a series of air pollution intensities, expressed in terms of pollution per employee for three digit industries. After converting these intensities into tons per 1987 dollar (and other adjustments for minor errors and inconsistencies, see Aguayo et al. 2001), these coefficients are divided by the IPPS coefficients for the United States. As might be expected, the majority of Mexican industry is dirtier per unit of output in Mexico than in the United States (Gallagher 2002). Interestingly, a handful of key industries, iron and steel, non-ferrous metals, and cement are actually cleaner per unit of output in Mexico relative to the United States (analyzing why this occurs is the subject of Chapter 5).

Chapter 4

Chapter 4 uses newly corrected air pollution data for Mexico to examine the scale and composition effects of economic integration on Mexican manufacturing. This part of the appendix explains the calculations involved in adjusting the data and then outlines how the empirical investigations in Chapter 4 were carried out.

Adjusting the World Bank Pollution Intensities for Mexico

The author was involved in an effort to "correct" the World Bank's data. These notes are based on a paper the author wrote with two Mexican colleagues, Franisco Aguayo of the Program on Science, Technology and Development at El Colegio de Mexico and Anna Citlalic Gonzalez of INE: "Dirt is in the Eye of the Beholder: The World Bank Air Pollution Intensities for Mexico," (Aguayo, et al., 2001). There are three limitations relating to the newer World Bank air pollution intensities for Mexico. First, a size bias was introduced into the calculation of the overall coefficients that are most usable for researchers and that were used in previous studies. Second, a number of technical errors were made in the construction of the database. Third, the expression of the data in terms of pollution per employee is problematical because employment is not an adequate measure of economic activity, especially in the Mexican case.

Regarding the size bias, the World Bank sample does not represent the size distribution of Mexican industry well enough to serve as a proxy for Mexican industry as a whole. The World Bank sample includes an abundance of large firms. Only 40 percent of the World Bank sample contains smaller firms, representing under two percent of employment in the sample. According to the Mexican Industrial Census, over 93 percent of all firms are small, and account for just under 15 percent of industrial employment.

The second limitation of the World Bank Mexico intensities are a number of technical errors and inconsistencies. Different errors in the intensities for the footwear industry, wood furniture, oil, and tobacco industries render them unusable. For large firms in the shoe industry (code 324), emissions for each pollutant are recorded to be exactly the same (to the 19th significant figure) for all five criteria pollutants. These appear to by typographical errors. The same occurred for large firms in the wood furniture industry for particulate matter (PT) and hydrocarbons (HC). It is impossible for firms to emit exactly the same amount of pollution across pollutants. Regarding oil refining, the World Bank intensities report coefficients for small and medium sized firms although, according to the census, such firms do not exist in Mexico. Finally, there are no recorded coefficients for small or medium sized firms in the Tobacco industry. One would think that the overall coefficient would then equal the coefficient for large firms; however, the overall coefficients for tobacco are the coefficients for large firms multiplied by a factor of 1.03.

The third shortcoming of the World Bank intensities for Mexico is that they are expressed in terms of pollution per employee rather than in terms of pollution per unit of output or value added. The World Bank is aware that this is not the ideal measure. Indeed, the World Bank has said the "volume of output would be the ideal unit of measurement" (Hettige et al. 1994). However, they chose to create intensities in this manner with a plausible rationale—employment data is more prevalent in developing countries and would thus be easier to use by analysts. This becomes a problem, particularly for Mexico.

When thinking about the relationship between economic activity and pollution, it is important to remember that it is not workers who create pollution, but rather the processes which they operate during production. Similarly, levels of employment are not measures of economic performance. In fact, they can vary independently from levels of output. In a country such as Mexico, such inconsistencies can be pronounced. During periods of economic transformation (such as that experienced by Mexico from 1985 to 1999), firms can shed workers to maintain productivity, and do so without changing their production techniques in any manner that might affect pollution levels. In such cases, using pollution per employee measures may be tracking large employment changes rather than changes in production processes. This problem becomes evident when looking at the following equation:

1) $$\frac{P}{L} = \frac{P}{Y} * \frac{Y}{L}$$

In this equation let P equal pollution, Y equal output, and L equal the number of employees. The expression P/L is the World Bank pollution intensity, and Y/L is worker productivity. P/Y is pollution per unit of output, the appropriate measure of intensity. When productivity is growing, constant pollution per employee can mean falling pollution per unit of output.

In our paper on these intensities, we compared estimates of pollution intensity in the Mexican steel industry between 1988 and 1993 using both methods. During the late 1980s, the steel industry in Mexico was privatized, resulting in the release of over 30,000 employees. Between 1988 and 1993, employment fell by 50 percent, while output rose by 15 percent. If pollution per employee is constant, total emissions fell sharply; if pollution depends on output, total emissions increased.

Finally, in the calculation of the pollution per employee estimates, another technical error was made. The World Bank confused production workers as they are called in the National System and Information for

Fixed Sources (SNIFF)—or "obreros" in Spanish—with employees ("empleados"). SNIFF does not record the number of employees but the number of production workers. The World Bank coefficients are thus really pollution per production worker, but are reported as pollution per employee.

Adjusting the World Bank Air Pollution Intensities for Mexico

To alleviate some of the problems identified in the previous section we adjusted the overall intensities to reflect the size distribution of Mexican industry, then we converted the pollution per employee estimates to pollution per value added coefficients.

As indicated in the previous section, the World Bank coefficients for Mexico under-represent the share of small firms in the Mexican economy. We estimate that the World Bank took the weighted average of the size distribution of plants in their sample to create their overall coefficients. To correct for this mistake, we took the weighted average of the size distribution of firms (weighted by the number of production workers) in the entire Mexican economy. This correction adjusts the coefficients closer to the intensities of the smaller firms. This affected some intensities dramatically, but not all of them. In sectors with fewer small firms, such as pulp and paper, other chemicals, non-ferrous metals, and the automotive sector, there was little change. In others, such as the food and beverage industry, and light machinery, the change was more pronounced.

We corrected for the pollution per employee problem in two ways. By obtaining a measure of production worker productivity we were able to convert the intensities into a measure of pollution per unit of value added. With value added data per production branch and data on the number of production workers from the Census of Manufactures, we calculated such a productivity measure which we then divided by the World Bank's pollution per worker estimates (after correcting for the size bias). Put another way:

$$2) \qquad \frac{P}{Y} = \frac{\dfrac{P}{O}}{\dfrac{Y}{O}}$$

In this equation, P is equal to pollution, Y is equal to output, and O is equal to production workers ("obreros"). We did not calculate intensities for three of the four industries with irreconcilable technical errors identified in the last section (footwear, tobacco, and wood furniture). We did calculate a coefficient for oil refining, but only use it in one exercise that is described later. Thus, the new coefficients adjust for the size bias, correct the production worker mistake, and express the coefficients in terms of pollution per unit of output. They are available both in pesos and in U.S. dollars.

Calculating the Scale and Composition Effects in Mexican Industry, 1984 to 1998

With these new data in hand, the crux of the analysis in this paper comes in the calculation of the scale and composition effects of air pollution in Mexican industry from 1985 to 1998. Strutt and Anderson (2000) have formalized these concepts, and guide the methodological approach taken in this paper (Strutt 2000). These authors express the change in total pollution as a function of scale, composition, and technique:

1) $\Delta P = S + C + T$

Here, P is pollution, S is the scale effect, C is the composition effect, and T is the technology effect.

The scale contribution to pollution grows at the same rate as manufactures value added, and holds the compositional and technological changes of Mexican industry constant:

2) $S_{it} = P_{ib}\left(\dfrac{Y_{mt}}{Y_{mb}} - 1\right)$

In equation (2), S is the change in pollution due to scale, i is three-digit ISIC industrial sector, b is the base year (1994), m is manufacturing, and t is the year to be calculated, Y is value added. Value added and employment data come from the United Nations Industrial Development Organization (UNIDO) ISIC 3 database (UNIDO 2000).

Calculating the composition effect allows the various industrial sectors to grow at different rates, net of the scale effect and holding the technology effect constant. For this reason, the composition effect in the base year will be zero (here C is the pollution due to composition, holding scale and technique constant):

3) $C_{it} = P_{ib}\left(\dfrac{Y_{it}}{Y_{ib}} - \dfrac{Y_{mt}}{Y_{mb}}\right)$

Levels of pollution in a single year, net of the composition effect, are equal to the sum of scale levels of pollution added to the sum of composition levels of pollution (S + C). Because there is only one pollution coefficient for one base year (1994), the technique effect (T) cannot be calculated (the same, very serious limitation occurs in all the studies mentioned earlier in the paper). Intensities for pollution would have to be available for at least two different periods in time to estimate the technique effect. Thus, to calculate how pollution changed over a time period, net levels in one year are subtracted from pollution levels in a previous year. Specifically, net levels of pollution in 1998 are subtracted from net levels in 1984.

These calculations are done for sulfur oxides (SO_x), nitrous oxides (NO_x), and PT because, as Table 1 shows, manufacturing is a key polluter of such pollutants. And, they are pollutants where data exists in Mexico.

Chapter 5

Chapter 5 compares the air pollution intensity of U.S. and Mexican manufacturing and attempts to explain the differences between the two. The comparison itself is defined as the Harmonization index, which is described below and followed by a description of the subsequent analysis conducted for the chapter.

Creating a Harmonization Index (HI)

The Harmonization Index (HI) is defined as the ratio of air pollution intensity per industry in Mexico, to that of the United States. If the emissions intensity is close to parity for the two countries, then the harmonization index would be close to one—implying that intensity levels had essentially harmonized between the two countries. This can be expressed in the following manner:

$$H = \frac{1}{3}\left[\frac{(SO_x/Y)\,Mex}{(SO_x/Y)US} + \frac{(NO_x/Y)Mex}{(NO_x/Y)US} + \frac{(PT/Y)Mex}{(PT/Y)US}\right]$$

Where the harmonization index is (H), value added is (Y), Mexican industries are (Mex), and the U.S. is (US). This exercise is conducted for the eight largest industries in Mexico where there is comparable data on energy and fuel use that is used in the subsequent calculations. These industries comprise 65 percent of Mexican manufacturing in terms of value added. As in the previous chapter, coefficients for the U.S. are from the Industrial Pollution Projection System. Coefficients for Mexico are the adjusted World Bank air pollution intensities that are described and used in the previous chapter as well. Production data for both countries are from the United Nations Industrial Development Organization.

Because the U.S. coefficients are in 1987 dollars, the Mexico coefficients require currency conversion. The Mexico coefficients (in 1992 pesos) are converted to 1987 dollars with the GDP deflator. The new intensities in dollars for Mexico are then divided by the U.S. intensities for each pollutant in each industry. Finally, an average of all the ratios for all three pollutants is taken.

Regression Analysis for Chapter 5

A regression experiment was conducted for chapter 5 that attempts to statistically examine the hypotheses discussed in that chapter. Given that data is not available to conduct a full analysis, these experiments are speculative, and should only be seen to supplement the discussion in chapter 5. Nevertheless, these statistical experiments do lend support to the findings in that chapter.

Model 1 Regressions

Regression analysis can be applied to examine the air pollution intensities in Mexico and the United States. Working from the framework pertaining to the major determinants of air pollution in industry that was described above, Model 1 shows that pollution intensity can be a function of energy intensity and byproduct emissions intensity:

Model 1

$$\text{a.} \quad \frac{P}{Y} = k\frac{X}{Y} + \frac{B}{Y}$$

where (P) is air pollution measured in tons of pollution, (Y) is value added, (X) is energy use in megajoules, (B) are the byproduct emissions uncorrelated with energy, (k) is a constant to express average tons of pollution per megajoule of energy. In this model, pollution intensity is regressed on energy intensity and byproduct intensity for each country and industry.

Comparable data on byproduct emissions does not exist for each country. Therefore, in regressions for Model 1, this model must be adapted in the following manner (using lower case letters to substitute for intensity):

Model 1

    b. $p = kx + \bar{b} + \varepsilon$

then:

$$p = k(x + b^*) \quad \left(\text{if } b^* = \frac{\bar{b}}{k} \right)$$

or in natural logarithms:

$$\ln p = \ln k + \ln(x + b^*)$$

Here $(\bar{b})$ is the mean value of byproduct intensity. This equation expresses Model 1 with natural logarithms to account for the wide variation among sectors. There are two possible solutions to this equation. First, if the mean value of byproduct emissions is zero, then the slope of the constant term should be one for each country—implying that for every one percent increase in energy use there is a corresponding increase in pollution. However, if the mean value of byproduct emissions does not equal zero (in other words, the equation for Model 1 b. is the true relationship), the slope of the constant term will be less than one—implying that byproduct emissions change less than proportionally to energy emissions. The version of Model 1 that is estimated then, is:

Model 1

    c. $\ln p = \alpha + \beta \ln x$

Where alpha is the constant term and beta is the coefficient (slope) to be estimated. Comparable energy use, fuel use, and production data are available for each of the eight industries in Mexico and the United States. Mexico's National Energy Balance provides energy and fuel use data (INEGI, various years). These data, expressed in megajoules, are divided by value added data from Mexico's Industrial Census, converted into 1993 U.S. dollars (INEGI, 1998). For the U.S., the Census of Manufactures provides energy and fuel use in trillions of British Thermal Units (btus). These data are converted to megajoules and then merged with U.S. Census data for value added to express energy intensities in megajoules per 1993 U.S. dollar as well. For Mexico, the average intensity from 1988 to 1994 was taken (the primary years that comprise the air pollution data), for the US intensity for 1991 was used because of its proximity to the 1987 IPPS coefficients. The results of this exercise are presented below.

Table A.1 exhibits regression results for Models 1 and 2 that are described in the appendix. The Model 1 regression results indicate that in the United States, energy and criteria air pollution are strongly correlated, but in Mexico there are significant byproduct emissions that rise less than proportionally to energy. This is shown by the fact that the coefficient for energy intensity for the United States is very close to one, or 1.04. Referring back to the equation Model 1 c. then, here the mean value of byproduct emission intensity is zero. This is not the case in Mexico, as the coefficient (0.35) is less than one—as predicted above. In Mexico, byproduct emissions are significantly important and not always correlated with energy use.

TABLE **A.1**   Regression Results from Chapter 5

| X variables | Y Variable: Pollution Intensity | | | |
| | Model 1 | | Model 2 | |
	U.S.	Mexico	U.S.	Mexico
energy intensity	1.04	0.35		
	3.80	2.48		
clean intensity			0.87	0.39
			1.85	1.84
dirty intensity			0.20	0.01
			0.63	0.11
Adjusted R^2	0.66	0.42	0.53	0.44
N	8	8	8	8

Model 2 Regressions

A second set of regressions can be conducted and compared for each country. Each of these data sets also includes figures on fuel use. In Mexico, the primary energy sources are gas, diesel, residual fuel oil, and electricity. The United States uses the same energy inputs, in addition to coal. Indeed, coal comprises 10 percent of all energy inputs into U.S. industry, reaching as high as 49 percent of the fuel used for iron and steel making (DOE, 1991). Table 5.2 exhibited emissions factors for the various fuels used in Mexico, and the emissions factor for coal use in the United States (where the heat content of coal is assumed to be 18,360 megajoules per cubic meter).

In Mexico, the two fuels that are the most air pollution intensive are residual fuel oil and diesel. Coal is very air pollution intensive in the United States. A second set of regressions are conducted to determine the extent to which fuel use determines the levels of air pollution intensity in the two countries. Model 2 is expressed as:

Model 2

$$\frac{P}{Y} = a\frac{C}{Y} + b\frac{D}{Y}$$

where (a) and (b) are coefficients to be estimated, (D) are the dirty fuels used for each industry (sum of coal, residual fuel oil, and diesel), and (C) are clean fuels (gas and electricity). This regression is run for both Mexico and the United States. The coefficients (a) and (b) will be compared for the two countries. As in the case of the first regressions, one would expect that these coefficients could be equal in each country.

The Model 2 regressions, that regress pollution intensity on the intensity of clean and dirty fuels in each industry, do not yield significant results. Referring back to Table 5.3, for both the United States and for Mexico, the fuel mix does not seem to be significantly correlated with the amount of pollution intensity for each industry. For clean industries, the sign of the coefficient is what one would expect. One would expect the sign for each variable to be positive, but that the coefficient for dirty fuels would be bigger. In each case for each country the sign is positive for clean industries, indicating that as the quantity of clean fuels increases in an industry so does pollution intensity. However, for neither country are the relationships statistically significant.

Perhaps the fundamental explanation for these results are the limited amount of data being analyzed. For each regression there were only eight observations, making regression analysis of limited use. While the Model 1 results indicate a clear relationship between energy and pollution intensity, the Model 2 results do not indicate a relationship between fuel mix and pollution.

Bibliography

Aguayo, F. and K. Gallagher (2001). Dirt is in the Eye of the Beholder: The World Bank Air Pollution Intensities for Mexico. Medford, MA, Tufts University.

Alfie-Cohen, M. (1998). Y El Desierto Se Volvio Verde: Movimientos Ambientalistas Binacionales. Azcapotzalco, Universidad IberoAmericana.

Anderson, K. (1992). The standard welfare economics of policies affecting trade and the environment. *The Greening of World Trade Issues*. K. Anderson and R. Blackhurst. Ann Arbor, The University of Michigan Press.

Audley, J. (1996). *Green Politics and Global Trade: NAFTA and the Future of Environmental Politics*. Washington D.C., Georgetown University Press.

Baker and McKenzie (2000). *Environmental Law and Policy in Latin America*. Washington, Baker and McKenzie.

Bank, W. (1992). *World Development Report*. Washington, International Bank for Reconstruction and Development.

Barbier, E. B. (1994). Natural Capital and the Economics of Environment and Development. *Investing in Natural Capital: The Ecological Economics Approach to Sustainability*. J. A. et al. Washington, Island Press.

Barkin, D. (1999). *The Greening of Business in Mexico*, UNRISD.

Bartzokas, A. and M. Yarime (1997). Technology Trends in Pollution-Intensive Industries: A Review of Sectoral Trends. The Netherlands, United Nations University.

Baumol, W. J. and W. E. Oates (1998). *The Theory of Environmental Policy*. New York, Cambridge University Press.

Blackman, A., et al. (2001). The Greening of Development Economics. Washington, Resources for the Future.

Brown, F. (2000). Environmental Performance and Trade Liberalization in the Mexican Textile Industry. *Industry and Environment in Latin America*. R. Jenkins. London, Routledge.

CANACERO (2002). 1991–2000, Ten Years of Steelmaking Statistics. Col. del Valle, Mexico, CANACERO.

CEMEX (2002). www.cemex.com, CEMEX.

Crompton, P. (2001). "The Diffusion of New Steelmaking Technology." *Resources Policy* 27: 87–95.

Dasgupta, S., H. Hettige, et al. (2000). "What Improves Environmental Compliance? Evidence from Mexican Industry." *Journal of Environmental Economics and Management* 38: 39–66.

DOE, U.S.D.o.E. (2002). Environmental Overview, Mexico. http://www.fe.doe.gov/international/mexiover.html#Environmental, DOE.

Dominquez-Villalabos, L. (2000). Environmental performance in the Mexican chemical fibres industry in the context of an open market. *Industry and Environment in Latin America*. R. Jenkins. New York, Routledge: 190–217.

Dua, A. a. D. E. (1997). *Sustaining the Asia Pacific Miracle*. Washington, Institute for International Economics.

Dumas, E. (1996). Environmental Non-Governmental Networks: The Mexican Case in Theory and Practice. New Haven, CT, Yale University.

(EPA), United States Environmental Protection Agency Boder XXI web site.

Eskeland, G. S. and A. E. Harrison (1997). Moving to Greener Pastures? Multinationals and the Pollution Haven Hypothesis. *Trade, Global Policy, and the Environment*. P. G. Fredriksson. Washington, D.C., World Bank.

Esty, D. C. (1994). *Greening the GATT: Trade, Environment, and the Future*. Washington D.C., Institute for International Economics.

Esty, D. C. (1997). Environmental Protection during the Transition to a Market Economy. *Economies in Transition: Comparing Asia and Europe*. S. P. Wing Thye Woo, Jeffrey Sachs. Cambridge, MIT Press.

Esty, D. C. (1999). Economic Integration and the Environment. *The Energy Journal*. N. J. Vig and R. Axelrod. Washington, DC, CQ Press.

Esty, D. C. (2001). "Bridging the Trade and Environment Divide." *Journal of Econonomic Perspectives* 15: 113–130.

Evans, P. (1995). *Embedded Autonomy: States and Industrial Transformation*. Princeton, NJ, Princeton University Press.

Fields, G. (1995). Income Distributrion in Developing Countries: Conceptual, Data, and Policy Issues. *Critical Issues in Asian Development*. M. G. Quibria. Hong Kong, Oxford University Press: 75–93.

Gallagher, K. (2002). Industrial Pollution in Mexico: Did NAFTA Matter? Greening to Americas: NAPTA's Lessons for Hemispheric Trade C. Deere and D. C. Esty. Cambridge, MA, MIT Press.

Gentry, B. and L. Fernandez (1998). Mexican Steel. *Private Capital Flows and the Environment: Lessons from Latin America*. B. Gentry and E. Elgar.

Gilbreath, J. (2003). *Environment and Development in Mexico*. Washington, DC, Center for Strategic International Studies.

Gilbreath, J. and J. B. Torra (1994). The Environment: Unwelcome Guest at the Free Trade Party. *The NAFTA Debate*. M. D. Baer and S. Weintraub. Boulder, Lynn Rienner Publishers.

Grossman, G. M. and A. B. Krueger (1993). Environmental Impacts of a North American Free Trade Agreement. *The Mexico-US Free Trade Agreement*. P. Garber, MIT Press.

Hartman, R. S., D. Wheeler, et al. (1994). The Cost of Air Pollution Abatement, Center for Economic Studies, U.S. Bureau of the Census.

Hettige, H. e. a. (2000). "Industrial Pollution in Economic Development: The Environmental Kuznets Curve Revisited." *Journal of Development Economics* 62 (2).

Hettige, H., P. Martin, et al. (1994). The Industrial Pollution Projection System, World Bank.

Horvatth, R. (1997). Energy Consumption and the Environmental Kuznets Curve Debate. Department of Geography, University of Sydney, Sydney, NSW.

Hufbauer, G. C., et al., Ed. (2000). *NAFTA and the Environment: Seven Years Later*. Washington, D.C., Insitute for International Economics.

Husted, B. W. and J. M. Logsdon (1997). "The Impact of NAFTA on Mexico's Environmental Policy." *Growth and Change* 28 (Winter 1997): 24–48.

INE (1996). Inventario de Emisiones a la atmosfera en la ZMVM, Mexico. Mexico City, INE.

INE/SEMARNAP (1999). Primer Informe Nacional de Emisiones Y Tranferencias de Contaminantes, 1997–1998. Mexico City, RETC.

INEGI (National Institue of Statistics, G., and Informatics) (2000). Web site: www.inegi.gob.mx, (National Institue of Statistics, Geographics, and Informatics).

INEGI (2000). Sistema de Cuentas Economicas y Ecologicas de Mexico, 1993–1999. Aguascalientes, Instituto Nacional De Estadistica Geografia e Informatica.

IPCC (2001). *Climate Change 2001*. Geneva, World Meteorological Organization.

Jaffe, A., S. R. Peterson, and R. Stavins (1995). "Environmental Regulation and the Competitiveness of US Manufacturing." *Journal of Economic Literature* 33: 132–163.

Jayadevappa, R. and S. Chhatre (2000). "International Trade and Environmental Quality: A Survey." *Ecological Economics* 32: 77–95.

Jenkins, R. (1998). "Globalizacion y Contaminacion Industrial en Mexico y Malasia." *Comercio Exterior* 48 (12).

Kahn, M. E. (2001). United States Pollution Intensive Trade Trends From 1972 to 1992. Medford, MA, Tufts University.

Kaufmann, R. (1998). "The Determinants of Atmospheric SO_2 Concentrations: Reconsidering the Environmental Kuznets Curve." *Ecological Economics* 25 (2): 209–20.

Levinson, A. (1999). An Industry-Adjusted Index of State Environmental Compliance Costs. Cambridge, National Bureau of Economic Research.

List, J., Gallet, Craig (1999). "The Environmental Kuznets Curve: Does One Size Fit All?" *Ecological Economics* 31 (3): 473–480.

Lucas, R. E. B., et al. (1992). Economic Development, Environmental Regulation, and the International Migration of Toxic Industrial Pollution. *International Trade and the Environment*. P. Low. Washington, World Bank.

Mani, M. and D. Wheeler (1999). In Search of Pollution Havens? Dirty Industry in the World Economy. *Trade, Global Policy, and the Environment*. P. Fredrikkson. Washington, World Bank.

Marc-Johnson, P. and A. Beaulieu (1997). The Environment and NAFTA. Washington D.C., Island Press.

Margulis, S. (1996). Back-of the Envelope Estimate of Environmental Damage Costs in Mexico. *Pricing the Planet: Economic Analysis for Sustainable Development*. P. May. New York, Columbia University.

Mayer, F. (1998). *Interpreting NAFTA: The Science and Art of Political Analysis*. New York, Columbia University.

Mercado Garcia, A., Ed. (1999). *Instrumentos Economicos Para Un Comportamiento Empresarial Favorable Al Amiente En Mexico*. Camino al Ajusco, Mexico, El Colegio de Mexico.

Middlebrook, K. and Eduardo Zepeda (2003). *Confronting Development: Assessing Mexico's Economic and Social Policy Challenges*. Palo Alto, Stanford University Press.

Molina, L. and M. Molina (2002). *Air Quality in the Mexico Megacity*. Dordrecht, Kluwer Academic.

Mumme, S. (1998). Environmental Politics and Policy in Mexico. *Ecological Policy and Politics in Developing Countries*. U. Desai. Albany, State University of New York Press.

Mumme, S., R. Bath, et al. (1988). "Political Development and Environmental Policy in Mexico." *Latin American Research Review* XXIII (1).

North American Commission for Environmental Cooperation. (2002). Web site: www.cec.org.

Nadal, A. (2001). *The Environmental and Social Impacts of Economic Liberalization in Corn Production*. Washington, World Wildlife Fund.

Neumayer, E. (2001). *Greening Trade and Investment*. London, Earthscan.

Nordstrom, V. (1999). Trade and Environment. Geneva, World Trade Organization, WTO.

North, D. (1987). "Institutions, Transaction Costs, and Economic Growth." *Economic Inquiry 25*.

OECD (1998). *Environmental Performance Review for Mexico*. Paris, OECD.

Panayotou, T. (1993). *Green Markets: The Economics of Sustainable Development*. San Francisco, ICS Press.

Panayotou, T. (1997). "Demystifying the Environmental Kuznets Curve." *Environment and Development Economics* 2 (4): 451–463.

Panayotou, T. (1998). *Instruments of Change: Motivating and Financing Sustainable Development*. London, Earthscan.

Panayotou, T. (2000). Economic Growth and the Environment. Cambridge, MA, Center for International Development at Harvard Univeristy.

Panayotou, T. (2000). Globalization and Environment. Cambridge, MA, Harvard University, CID.

Porter, G. (1999). "Trade Competition and Pollution Standards: 'Race to the Bottom' or 'Stuck at the Bottom'?" *Journal of Environment & Development* 8 (2): 133–151.

(PROFEPA), (2000). Web site: www.profepa.gov.mx.

Quist, D. and I. H. Chapela (2001). Transgenic DNA introgressed into traditional maize landraces in Oaxaca, Mexico. *Nature*. 414.

Repetto, R. (1989). *Wasting Assets: Natural Resources in the National Income Accounts*. Washington, World Resources Institute.

Reppelin-Hill, V. (1999). "Trade and Environment: An Empirical Analysis of the Technology Effect in the Steel Industry." *Journal of Environmental Economics and Management* 38: 283–301.

Rodrik, D. (2001). The Global Governance of Trade As If Development Really Mattered. New York, United Nations Development Programme (UNDP).

Rodrik, D., Arvind Subramanian (2002). "Institutions Rule: The Primacy of Institutions over Geography and Integration in Economic Development." *NBER Working Paper 9305*.

Runge, C. F. (1995). Trade, Pollution, and Environmental Protection. *The Handbook of Environmental Economics*. D. W. Bromley. Cambridge, MA, Blackwell.

Schatan, C. (2002). Mexico's Manufacturing Exports and the Environment Under NAFTA. *The Environmental Effects of Free Trade*. Montreal, North American Commission for Environmental Cooperation.

Seldon, T. and D. Song (1994). "Environmental Quality and Development: Is there a Kuznets Curve for Air Pollution?" *Journal of Environmental Economics and Management* 27: 147–162.

Semarnap (2000). *Almanaque de Datos y Tendencias de la Calidad del Aire en Ciudades Mexicanas.* Mexico City.

Serafy, S. E. (1993). Depletable Resources: Fixed Capital or Inventories? *Approaches to Environmental Accounting.* A. a. C. S. Franz, Physica-Verlag Heidelberg.

Shafik, N. (1994). "Economic Development and Environmental Quality." *Oxford Economic Papers* 46: 757–773.

Smil, V. a. M. Y. (1998). *The Economic Costs of China's Environmental Degradation.* Cambridge, American Academy of Arts and Sciences.

Smith, M. (1997). *The U.S. Paper Industry and Sustainable Production.* Cambridge, MA, MIT Press.

Stern, D. (1998). "Progress on the Environmental Kuznets Curve?" *Environment and Development Economics* 3: 173–196.

Stern, D., Michael, Common (2001). "Is There an Environmental Kuznets Curve for Sulfur?" *Journal of Environmental Economics and Management* 41 (2): 162–178.

Sterner, T. (1990). "Energy Efficiency and Capital Embodied Technical Change: The Case of Mexican Cement Maufacturing." *The Energy Journal* 11 (2): 155–167.

Stiglitz, J. (1989). "Markets, Market Failure, and Development." *American Economic Review* 79.

Strutt, A. and Anderson Kym (2000). "Will Trade Liberalization Harm the Environment? The Case of Indonesia to 2020." *Environmental and Resource Economics* 17 (3): 203–32.

Suri, V. and Chapman (1998). "Economic Growth, Trade and Energy: Implications for the Environmental Kuznets Curve." *Ecological Economics* 25 (2).

Tellus Institute (1992). CSG/Tellus Packaging Study: Assessing the impacts of production and disposal of packaging and public policy measures to alter its mix. Boston, The Council of State Governments, and U.S. Environmental Protection Agency, New Jersy Department of Environmental Protection and ENergy.

Ten Kate, A. (1993). Industrial Development and the Environment in Mexico. Washington D.C., World Bank.

Texas Center for Policy Studies (1997). Burning Our Health: Hazardous Waste Incineration in Cement Kilns. Austin, Texas Center for Policy Studies.

Torras, M. and James Boyce (1996). "Income, Inequality, and Pollution: A Reassessment of the Environmental Kuznets Curve." *Ecological Economics.*

U.S. Department of Energy (1997). Energy and Environmental Profile of U.S. Aluminum Industry. Columbia, MD, U.S. Dept. of Energy, Office of Industrial Technologies.

UNCTAD (2002). Country Fact Sheet: Mexico, from World Investment Report 2002: Transnational Corporations and Export Competitiveness. New York, United Nations.

UNIDO (2000). Demand and Supply Database. Geneva, United Nations Industrial Development Organization.

UNIDO (2000). Industrial Statistics Database. Geneva, United Nations Industrial Development Organization.

Unruh, G. and W. Moomaw (1997). "An Alternative Analysis of the Apparent EKC Relationship." *Ecological Economics.*

Vijay, S. (2001). Non-Transportation Energy-Related Sources of Air Pollution in the MCMA: Emission Implications and Mitigation Options. Cambridge, Massachusetts Institute of Technology.

Vincent, J. R. (1997). "Testing for Environmental Kuznets Curves Within a Developing Country." *Environment and Development Economics* 2 (4): 417–431.

Weiner, T. (2002). U.S. Will Get Power, and Pollution from Mexico. *New York Times:* A3.

Whalley, J. a. B. Z. (2001). "What Could a World Environmental Organization Do?" *Global Environmental Politics* 1:1(February).

Winfield, P. (2003). PRTR as an Example of Harmonization of Standards. *Greening NAFTA.* John Knox and David Markel, Eds. Palo Alto, Stanford University Press.

Wise, T., Hilda Salazar, and Laura Carlsen (2003). *Confronting Globalization: Popular Resistance and Economic Integration in Mexico.* West Hartford, Kumerian Press.

World Bank (1992). *World Development Report.* Washington, International Bank for Reconstruction and Development.

World Bank (1997). *Clear Water, Blue Skies.* Washington, World Bank.

World Bank (2001). *Mexico: A Comprehensive Development Agenda.* Washington, D.C., World Bank.

World Bank (2002). New Ideas in Pollution Regulation, International Bank for Reconstruction and Development.

Zarsky, L. (1997). Stuck in the Mud? Nation-States, Globalisation and the Environment. *Globalisation and the Environment, Preliminary Perspectives.* Paris, OECD.

Index